Tropical Paradise: Exotic Cocktails to Transport Drinkers

Copyright Page

TITLE: Tropical Paradise: Exotic Cocktails to Transport Drinkers

1ST Edition

ISBN: 9798223620006

Table of Contents

Tropical Paradise: Exotic Cocktails to Transport Drinkers

By Roberto Miguel Rodriguez

1

Chapter 1: Classic Cocktails: A Bartender's Guide

The History of Classic Cocktails

In the world of mixology, classic cocktails hold a special place. These timeless concoctions have been enjoyed by generations of drinkers, and their origins can be traced back to some of the most iconic moments in cocktail history. Let's take a journey through time as we explore the fascinating history of classic cocktails.

The origins of classic cocktails can be found in the early days of bartending, when skilled mixologists experimented with different combinations of spirits, mixers, and garnishes. These pioneers laid the foundation for the cocktails we know and love today.

One of the earliest classic cocktails is the Old Fashioned. Dating back to the early 19th century, this simple yet elegant drink was originally made with whiskey, sugar, water, and a dash of bitters. Over the years, variations of the Old Fashioned emerged, but the basic recipe remains a staple in the cocktail world.

Another iconic classic cocktail is the Martini. This sophisticated drink became popular in the late 19th century and is traditionally made with gin and vermouth. The Martini has inspired countless variations, including the famous Vodka Martini, which gained popularity in the mid-20th century.

The Mojito, a refreshing rum-based cocktail, has its roots in Cuba. This classic drink was born in the 16th century and was initially consumed for its medicinal properties. Over time, the Mojito evolved into a beloved cocktail, featuring a delightful combination of rum, lime juice, sugar, mint leaves, and soda water.

As the cocktail culture continued to evolve, new classics emerged. The Cosmopolitan, made famous by the television series "Sex and the City," is a perfect example. This vodka-based cocktail combines cranberry juice, lime juice, triple sec, and a splash of citrus-flavored vodka for a vibrant and flavorful drink.

Classic cocktails not only have historical significance but also serve as a foundation for modern mixology. Many contemporary cocktails are inspired by the classics, with bartenders putting their own unique spin on the traditional recipes.

Whether you're a fan of whiskey, gin, rum, vodka, or any other spirit, there's a classic cocktail to suit your taste. From the traditional Old Fashioned to the tropical Mojito, these timeless drinks have stood the test of time and continue to delight drinkers around the world.

So, raise your glass and toast to the rich history of classic cocktails. Cheers to the mixologists of the past and the bartenders of today who keep these beloved libations alive.

Essential Tools and Techniques for Making Classic Cocktails

Introduction:

Aspiring mixologists and cocktail enthusiasts, welcome to the subchapter on "Essential Tools and Techniques for Making Classic Cocktails" from the book "Tropical Paradise: Exotic Cocktails to Transport Drinkers." In this section, we will explore the fundamental tools and techniques every bartender or home mixologist should master to create the perfect classic cocktails that will transport you to tropical bliss. Whether you are a fan of classic cocktails, tropical delights, or signature drinks, this guide is tailored to meet the needs of all drink enthusiasts. So, let's dive into the world of mixology!

Tools of the Trade:

To create spectacular cocktails, you need the right tools. Here are the essential tools every bartender should have in their arsenal:

1. Cocktail Shaker: The workhorse of mixology, a shaker helps blend ingredients and chill the drink simultaneously.

2. Mixing Glass: Ideal for stirring cocktails gently, maintaining the clarity of spirits and delicate flavors.

3. Jigger: A must-have for precise measuring and ensuring the perfect balance of ingredients.

4. Bar Spoon: Used for stirring cocktails, layering ingredients, and muddling herbs or fruits.

5. Strainer: Essential for separating the drink from ice or any solids during pouring.

6. Muddler: Perfect for releasing the flavors of fruits, herbs, or spices by gently crushing them.

7. Citrus Juicer: For extracting fresh juice from lemons, limes, and oranges, adding a vibrant touch to your cocktails.

Mastering Techniques:

Now that you have the right tools, let's explore some essential techniques for crafting classic cocktails:

1. Stirring: Learn the art of gently stirring cocktails to achieve a smooth and well-mixed drink.

2. Shaking: Master the vigorous shaking technique to create refreshing and vibrant cocktails.

3. Muddling: Understand the proper muddling technique to release the flavors of fruits, herbs, or spices.

4. Straining: Perfect your straining skills to ensure a clean and debris-free pour.

5. Garnishing: Discover creative garnishing techniques to elevate the visual appeal and aroma of your cocktails.

Conclusion:

Congratulations! You are now equipped with the essential tools and techniques required to create classic cocktails that will transport you to a tropical paradise. Whether you are a fan of whiskey, gin, rum, or vodka cocktails, this guide caters to every niche. For those seeking non-alcoholic options, explore our section on mocktails. And if you're looking to create seasonal or signature cocktails, we've got you covered too. So, gather your tools, master the techniques, and embark on a journey of mixology mastery. Cheers to creating unforgettable and exotic cocktails!

Remember to always drink responsibly.

Classic Martini Variations

The classic martini is a timeless cocktail that has been enjoyed by drinkers for decades. Its simple yet sophisticated combination of gin and vermouth has paved the way for countless variations that have become classics in their own right. In this subchapter, we will explore some of the most popular classic martini variations, each with its own unique twist.

First up is the Dirty Martini, a favorite among olive enthusiasts. This variation adds a splash of olive brine to the traditional martini, giving it a slightly salty and savory flavor. Garnished with a few olives, the Dirty Martini is a perfect choice for those looking to add a bit of pizzazz to their drink.

Next, we have the Gibson Martini, a variation that swaps out the olive garnish for a cocktail onion. This small change adds a touch of sweetness and tanginess to the martini, creating a delightful contrast to the dryness of the gin and vermouth. The Gibson Martini is a must-try for those seeking a unique twist on the classic.

For those who prefer a sweeter martini, the Vodka Martini is the perfect choice. This variation replaces gin with vodka, resulting in a smoother and less herbal flavor profile. Whether you prefer it shaken or stirred, the Vodka Martini is a versatile option that can be tailored to your personal taste.

If you're a fan of citrusy flavors, the Lemon Drop Martini is sure to satisfy. This variation combines vodka, lemon juice, and a touch of sweetness for a refreshing and tangy cocktail. Perfectly balanced with a sugared rim, the Lemon Drop Martini is a crowd-pleaser that is especially popular during the summer months.

Last but not least, we have the Espresso Martini, a variation that adds a jolt of caffeine to the classic martini. Made with vodka, coffee liqueur, and a shot of espresso, this variation is a favorite among coffee lovers. The Espresso Martini is a perfect choice for those looking to combine their love for coffee and cocktails.

Whether you're a fan of the classic martini or looking to explore new variations, these classic martini variations are sure to transport you to a tropical paradise. Cheers to the art of mixology and the endless possibilities of the martini!

Old Fashioned: A Timeless Classic

In the world of cocktails, trends come and go, but there is one drink that has stood the test of time: the Old Fashioned. This classic cocktail has been enjoyed by drinkers for centuries, and its popularity shows no signs of waning. In fact, it has become a must-have in every bartender's repertoire, from the classic cocktail bars to the trendy craft cocktail joints.

The Old Fashioned is a simple yet sophisticated drink that embodies the essence of a bygone era. It is made with just a few ingredients: whiskey, sugar, bitters, and a twist of citrus. The magic lies in the balance of these elements, resulting in a drink that is both bold and smooth, with a hint of sweetness and a touch of bitterness.

For the lovers of classic cocktails, the Old Fashioned is a staple. Its timeless appeal lies in its simplicity and versatility. Whether you prefer bourbon or rye whiskey, the Old Fashioned can be customized to suit your taste. Experiment with different types of bitters, such as orange or cherry, to add a unique twist. And for those who like to get creative, try muddling a cherry or an orange slice to enhance the flavors even further.

But the Old Fashioned isn't just for purists. It can also be a great base for tropical cocktails, adding a touch of sophistication to your exotic creations. Imagine sipping a Pineapple Old Fashioned on a tropical beach, or a Mango Old Fashioned at a summer barbecue. The possibilities are endless, and the results are always delicious.

For those who prefer non-alcoholic options, the Old Fashioned can be easily transformed into a refreshing mocktail. Simply replace the whiskey with a high-quality non-alcoholic spirit, such as Seedlip, and you'll have a drink that is just as satisfying as the original.

So, whether you're a fan of classic cocktails, tropical concoctions, or seasonal specialties, the Old Fashioned is a must-try. Its timeless appeal and versatility make it a true classic that will never go out of style. So raise your glass and enjoy the elegance and sophistication of this timeless cocktail. Cheers!

Manhattan: The Perfect Whiskey Cocktail

The Manhattan cocktail is a classic drink that exudes sophistication and elegance. It is the perfect blend of smooth whiskey, sweet vermouth, and aromatic bitters, creating a harmonious balance of flavors that will transport you to the bustling streets of Manhattan. Whether you're a whiskey enthusiast or just looking for a cocktail that embodies timeless style, the Manhattan is a must-try.

In this subchapter, we will explore the history, ingredients, and variations of the Manhattan cocktail. We will dive into the techniques used to create the perfect blend of flavors, as well as tips on how to personalize it to suit your taste preferences.

Originating in the late 19th century, the Manhattan has stood the test of time and remains a favorite among cocktail enthusiasts. It is said to have been created at the Manhattan Club in New York City for a banquet hosted by Lady Randolph Churchill, Winston Churchill's mother. Since then, it has become a staple in bars and speakeasies, captivating drinkers with its refined taste and allure.

The key ingredients of a classic Manhattan include rye whiskey, sweet vermouth, and aromatic bitters. However, there are variations that use bourbon or even Scotch whisky, allowing you to experiment and discover your preferred flavor profile. The combination of these ingredients creates a rich and complex drink that is sure to impress.

To create the perfect Manhattan, the right technique is crucial. From stirring the cocktail with ice to straining it into a chilled glass and garnishing it with a cherry, each step contributes to the overall presentation and taste. We will guide you through the process, ensuring that you master the art of cocktail making.

For those looking for a non-alcoholic alternative, we will also provide a mocktail version of the Manhattan. By substituting the whiskey with a non-alcoholic spirit and adjusting the other ingredients accordingly, you can still enjoy the flavors and experience of this iconic cocktail without the alcohol content.

Whether you're a fan of classic cocktails, tropical delights, or craft creations, the Manhattan cocktail offers a versatile and timeless option. Its roots in history, combined with its luxurious taste, make it a staple in the world of mixology. So, grab your shaker, select your preferred whiskey, and embark on a journey to Manhattan with this exquisite cocktail. Cheers!

Cosmopolitan: A Modern Twist on a Classic

In the world of cocktails, some drinks stand the test of time and become timeless classics. One such cocktail is the Cosmopolitan. Known for its vibrant pink hue and tangy flavor, the Cosmopolitan has been a favorite among drinkers for decades. But what if we told you there's a modern twist on this beloved classic that will transport you to a tropical paradise?

Introducing the Tropical Paradise Cosmopolitan – a refreshing and exotic take on the traditional Cosmo that will tantalize your taste buds and transport you to a sun-soaked beach. This modern twist combines the familiar flavors of cranberry juice, lime, and vodka with a tropical twist, such as a splash of pineapple juice or a hint of passion fruit. The result? A cocktail that's both familiar and exciting, perfectly suited for those looking to add a touch of the tropics to their drink repertoire.

For the lovers of classic cocktails, the Tropical Paradise Cosmopolitan offers a fresh and contemporary option that still retains the elegance and sophistication of the original. Its vibrant colors and tropical flavors will surely impress your guests at any gathering or soirée. Whether you're a seasoned bartender or a cocktail enthusiast, this recipe will become a staple in your repertoire.

For those who prefer tropical cocktails, the Tropical Paradise Cosmopolitan is a must-try. It combines the best of both worlds – the fruity and refreshing flavors of the tropics with the sophistication of a classic cocktail. Sip on this delightful concoction and let your mind wander to a sandy beach, swaying palm trees, and the sound of gentle waves crashing against the shore.

And let's not forget our friends who enjoy mocktails or non-alcoholic mixed drinks. The Tropical Paradise Cosmopolitan can easily be adapted to suit your preferences. Simply replace the vodka with a non-alcoholic spirit or a flavored syrup, and you'll have a mocktail that's just as delicious and refreshing.

Whether you're a fan of classic cocktails, tropical concoctions, or non-alcoholic drinks, the Tropical Paradise Cosmopolitan is a versatile and exciting choice. It's a modern twist on a classic that will transport you to a sun-soaked paradise with every sip. So go ahead, mix up a batch of this delightful cocktail, and let the flavors take you on a journey to a tropical oasis. Cheers to paradise in a glass!

Margarita: The Iconic Tequila Cocktail

The Margarita, with its refreshing blend of tart lime and smooth tequila, is undoubtedly one of the most iconic cocktails in the world. Originating in Mexico, this classic drink has gained popularity across the globe, becoming a staple in bars and beach resorts alike. In this subchapter, we dive into the history, ingredients, and variations of the Margarita, providing a comprehensive guide for both novice and seasoned bartenders.

To truly appreciate the Margarita, it's essential to understand its roots. Legend has it that the cocktail was first created in the late 1930s or early 1940s by a Mexican bartender named Carlos "Danny" Herrera. Seeking a refreshing drink for a customer who couldn't handle the harsh taste of straight tequila, Herrera combined tequila, lime juice, and a touch of orange liqueur, serving it over ice in a salt-rimmed glass. The Margarita was an instant hit, quickly spreading throughout Mexico and eventually finding its way to the United States.

The classic Margarita recipe calls for three key ingredients: tequila, lime juice, and orange liqueur. However, the beauty of this cocktail lies in its versatility, allowing for countless variations and flavor combinations. A skilled bartender can experiment with different tequila styles, such as blanco, reposado, or añejo, to create unique Margarita experiences. Additionally, fruit-infused variations, such as the popular strawberry or mango Margarita, add a delightful twist to this already beloved drink.

For those seeking a non-alcoholic option, the Mocktail version of the Margarita can be just as enjoyable. By substituting the tequila with a non-alcoholic spirit or simply omitting it altogether, bartenders can create a refreshing and flavorful virgin Margarita that satisfies even the most discerning palate.

The Margarita's versatility extends beyond its flavor profile, making it a perfect cocktail for different seasons and holidays. Bartenders can create seasonal Margaritas by incorporating fresh fruits and herbs that are abundant during specific times of the year. From a fiery Jalapeño Margarita for summer to a spiced Cranberry Margarita for the holiday season, the possibilities are endless.

Whether you're a fan of classic cocktails, tropical delights, or creative craft concoctions, the Margarita has something to offer. Its timeless appeal and adaptability make it a must-have in any bartender's repertoire. So, grab your shaker, rim that glass with salt, and transport yourself to a tropical paradise with a perfectly crafted Margarita in hand. Cheers!

Mojito: A Refreshing Rum Classic

When it comes to classic cocktails, there are few that can match the refreshing and vibrant flavors of the Mojito. Originating in Havana, Cuba, this timeless drink has become a favorite among drinkers all over the world. With its combination of rum, lime, mint, sugar, and soda water, the Mojito offers a perfect balance of sweet, tart, and herbaceous notes that truly transport you to a tropical paradise.

As part of our "Tropical Paradise: Exotic Cocktails to Transport Drinkers" book, we couldn't miss the opportunity to feature this beloved cocktail. Whether you're a seasoned bartender looking to expand your repertoire or a cocktail enthusiast eager to create your own tropical oasis at home, the Mojito is a must-have recipe in your arsenal.

For those who love the classics, "Classic Cocktails: A Bartender's Guide" and "Rum Cocktails: A Bartender's Guide" will appreciate the Mojito's timeless appeal. The combination of rum, typically white or silver, with fresh lime juice and muddled mint leaves creates a harmonious blend of flavors that is both invigorating and satisfying.

If you're a fan of tropical flavors, "Tropical Cocktails: A Bartender's Guide" and "Signature Cocktails: A Bartender's Guide" will surely catch your attention. The Mojito's zesty lime and refreshing mint perfectly complement the laid-back vibes of a beachside getaway, making it a go-to choice for those seeking a taste of the tropics.

For those who prefer non-alcoholic options, "Mocktails: A Bartender's Guide" offers a range of delicious non-alcoholic mixed drinks. The Mojito can easily be adapted into a mocktail by simply omitting the rum and replacing it with soda water or a non-alcoholic spirit alternative. This allows everyone to enjoy the vibrant flavors of the Mojito, regardless of their preference for alcohol.

In conclusion, the Mojito is a versatile cocktail that appeals to a wide range of drinkers. Whether you're a fan of classic cocktails, tropical flavors, or non-alcoholic options, the Mojito has something to offer. So sit back, relax, and let this refreshing rum classic transport you to a tropical paradise with every sip. Cheers!

Sidecar: A Sophisticated Brandy Cocktail

If you're a fan of classic cocktails and appreciate the artistry of mixology, then the Sidecar is a must-try. This sophisticated brandy cocktail has a rich history and a timeless appeal that will transport you to a tropical paradise with every sip. Whether you're a seasoned drinker or just starting to explore the world of cocktails, the Sidecar is a drink that should not be missed.

Originating in the early 20th century, the Sidecar is believed to have been created in Paris, France. It quickly gained popularity among the elite and became a staple in high-end bars and clubs. The recipe has since evolved, but the basic components remain the same – brandy, orange liqueur, and lemon juice.

To make the perfect Sidecar, start with a high-quality brandy. The rich and smooth flavors of the brandy are complemented by the sweetness of orange liqueur and the tartness of fresh lemon juice. The cocktail is typically served in a chilled glass with a sugar rim, adding a touch of sweetness to each sip.

The Sidecar is a versatile cocktail that can be adapted to suit different tastes. For those who prefer a sweeter drink, a splash of simple syrup can be added. If you're looking for a more tropical twist, try using a tropical fruit-flavored liqueur instead of the traditional orange liqueur. The possibilities are endless, allowing you to create a signature Sidecar that reflects your personal taste.

This cocktail is not only a favorite among classic cocktail enthusiasts but also a staple in tropical cocktail recipes. Its sophisticated flavors and refreshing qualities make it a perfect choice for those looking to escape to a tropical paradise, even if just for a moment. Whether you're sipping on a Sidecar by the beach or enjoying it at a holiday party, this cocktail is sure to transport you to a world of exotic flavors and tropical delights.

So, whether you're a fan of classic cocktails, tropical drinks, or seasonal delights, the Sidecar is a cocktail that should not be overlooked. Its sophisticated combination of brandy, orange liqueur, and lemon juice makes it a timeless favorite among bartenders and drink connoisseurs alike. So sit back, relax, and let the Sidecar whisk you away to a tropical paradise with its exotic flavors and tantalizing aromas. Cheers!

Daiquiri: A Tropical Rum Delight

Welcome to the subchapter "Daiquiri: A Tropical Rum Delight" from our book "Tropical Paradise: Exotic Cocktails to Transport Drinkers." This chapter is dedicated to all the cocktail enthusiasts who love to indulge in the world of flavors and tropical delights. Whether you're a bartender looking to expand your repertoire or a drinks aficionado seeking new recipes, this subchapter is perfect for you. Let's dive into the magical world of daiquiris!

The daiquiri is a classic cocktail that has stood the test of time. Originating in Cuba, it has become a staple in bars around the world. This delicious concoction is simple yet versatile, making it an ideal choice for any occasion.

In this subchapter, we will explore the history of the daiquiri and its evolution over the years. We will take you on a journey through the various iterations of this tropical rum delight, including the traditional lime daiquiri, as well as modern twists with fruits like strawberries, mangoes, and pineapples. You'll learn how to balance the flavors and create the perfect daiquiri every time.

For those who prefer non-alcoholic options, we haven't forgotten you! We will also introduce you to a range of mocktail daiquiris that capture the essence of the original recipe without the alcohol. These refreshing and flavorful mocktails are perfect for those who want to enjoy a tropical treat without the buzz.

Whether you're a fan of classic cocktails, tropical delights, or signature mixes, the daiquiri has something to offer everyone. We will also explore how to incorporate whiskey, gin, and vodka into your daiquiris, giving you an endless array of options to experiment with.

Additionally, we have included seasonal variations of the daiquiri that highlight the flavors of different seasons and holidays. From spicy pumpkin daiquiris for autumn to refreshing watermelon daiquiris for summer, you'll find a daiquiri for every occasion.

So, grab your shaker, rum, and tropical ingredients, and join us on this delightful journey through the world of daiquiris. Whether you're a seasoned bartender or a cocktail enthusiast, you're bound to find something to tantalize your taste buds in this subchapter. Cheers to the tropical rum delight that is the daiquiri!

Negroni: The Bitter Sweet Classic

In the world of classic cocktails, few drinks can rival the timeless elegance and bold flavors of the Negroni. With its perfect balance of bitterness, sweetness, and herbal complexity, this cocktail has become a staple in bars around the globe. Whether you're a seasoned drinker or a curious newbie, the Negroni is a must-try for any cocktail enthusiast.

The origins of the Negroni can be traced back to early 20th century Italy. It was created by Count Camillo Negroni, who wanted a stronger version of his favorite cocktail, the Americano. By replacing the soda water with gin, the Negroni was born. Since then, it has captured the hearts and palates of cocktail lovers everywhere.

What sets the Negroni apart is its unique combination of ingredients. Equal parts gin, Campari, and sweet vermouth are stirred together over ice, resulting in a vibrant and complex drink. The bitterness of the Campari is balanced by the sweetness of the vermouth, while the gin adds a botanical depth that ties it all together. The result is a cocktail that is both refreshing and sophisticated.

For those who prefer a milder version, the Negroni can be modified to suit individual tastes. By adjusting the ratios of the ingredients, or adding a splash of soda water, you can create a drink that is tailored to your preferences. And for those who prefer non-alcoholic options, fear not! There are plenty of mocktail versions of the Negroni that capture the essence of the original without the booze.

The Negroni is not only a classic cocktail, but it also lends itself to endless variations. Bartenders around the world have put their own spin on this beloved drink, experimenting with different spirits, bitters, and garnishes. From barrel-aged Negronis to smoked versions, there is a Negroni for every palate and occasion.

So, whether you're sipping a Negroni on a tropical beach or cozying up by the fireplace, this bittersweet classic is sure to transport you to a world of exotic flavors and timeless elegance. Cheers to the Negroni, the cocktail that continues to captivate drinkers and inspire bartenders worldwide.

Tom Collins: A Gin-Based Refreshment

If you're a fan of classic cocktails and are looking for a refreshing drink to transport you to a tropical paradise, then the Tom Collins is the perfect choice. This timeless cocktail has been a favorite among drinkers for decades, and it's easy to see why.

The Tom Collins is a gin-based drink that is both light and citrusy, making it the ideal choice for those hot summer days or tropical getaways. It is believed to have originated in the 19th century and has since become a staple in bars around the world.

To make a Tom Collins, you'll need just a few simple ingredients: gin, lemon juice, simple syrup, and club soda. Start by filling a Collins glass with ice cubes, then add 2 ounces of gin, 1 ounce of lemon juice, and 1/2 ounce of simple syrup. Give it a good stir to combine the flavors, then top it off with club soda. Garnish with a lemon slice or a cherry, and your Tom Collins is ready to be enjoyed.

What sets the Tom Collins apart from other gin-based cocktails is its light and bubbly nature. The addition of club soda gives it a refreshing effervescence that is perfect for those hot summer days by the pool or beach. It's a drink that you can sip on all day without feeling weighed down.

For bartenders looking to expand their repertoire, the Tom Collins is a must-have in their cocktail arsenal. It's a classic cocktail that never goes out of style, and its simplicity makes it easy to whip up for customers looking for a refreshing drink.

Whether you're a fan of classic cocktails, tropical concoctions, or signature drinks, the Tom Collins is a versatile choice that can be enjoyed by all. Its light and citrusy flavors make it a popular choice among gin lovers, and its refreshing qualities make it a go-to drink for those looking to cool down on a hot day.

So, the next time you're in the mood for a gin-based refreshment that will transport you to a tropical paradise, look no further than the Tom Collins. With just a few simple ingredients, you can create a drink that is sure to impress both yourself and your guests. Cheers!

Chapter 2: Tropical Cocktails: A Bartender's Guide

Introduction to Tropical Cocktails

Welcome to the world of tropical cocktails! In this subchapter, we will take you on a journey to a paradise of exotic flavors, vibrant colors, and refreshing concoctions. Whether you are a seasoned drinker or a curious beginner, this chapter is designed to transport you to the sunny beaches of the tropics with every sip.

For lovers of classic cocktails, tropical cocktails offer a delightful twist on timeless favorites. Imagine the smoothness of a Piña Colada, the tanginess of a Mai Tai, or the refreshing burst of a Mojito, all infused with the tropical flavors of pineapple, coconut, passion fruit, and more. These drinks, carefully crafted by skilled bartenders, will transport you to a beachside cabana, where the ocean breeze and the sound of waves complement your sipping experience.

For those seeking a taste of the islands, our tropical cocktails guide will introduce you to the signature drinks of the tropics. From the famous Blue Hawaiian to the exotic Zombie, each cocktail tells a story of the region it comes from, capturing the essence of its culture and traditions. You will learn about the history behind each drink, the ingredients that make it unique, and the techniques used to create the perfect balance of flavors.

If you prefer non-alcoholic options, our mocktails guide will provide you with a variety of refreshing and flavorful mixed drinks. These alcohol-free concoctions are perfect for those who want to enjoy the tropical vibes without the buzz. From virgin Piña Coladas to alcohol-free Mojitos, you can still indulge in the exotic flavors of the tropics while staying sober.

For enthusiasts of specific spirits, we have dedicated chapters to whiskey, gin, rum, and vodka cocktails. Each guide will explore the tropical variations of these spirits, showcasing their versatility and pairing them with tropical fruits, herbs, and spices. Discover the boldness of a tropical whiskey sour, the crispness of a gin and tonic with a tropical twist, or the smoothness of a rum punch blended with tropical fruits.

Finally, our seasonal cocktails guide will provide you with a collection of drinks tailored to different seasons and holidays. From summery tropical punches for poolside parties to spiced cocktails for cozy winter nights, you will find the perfect drink for every occasion.

So, grab your shaker, prepare your garnishes, and get ready to embark on a tropical adventure through the world of cocktails. Let the flavors of the tropics transport you to a paradise of taste and relaxation. Cheers to tropical cocktails!

Essential Ingredients for Tropical Cocktails

In the world of cocktails, few things evoke the feeling of paradise quite like tropical flavors. From the vibrant colors to the exotic ingredients, tropical cocktails have the power to transport drinkers to a beachside oasis with just one sip. Whether you're a fan of classic cocktails, signature creations, or even non-alcoholic mocktails, mastering the art of tropical mixology is a must for any bartender.

When it comes to crafting the perfect tropical cocktail, the right ingredients are essential. Here are some must-have elements to create a taste of the tropics:

1. Fresh Fruit: Nothing says tropical like the juicy sweetness of fresh fruit. Pineapple, mango, passionfruit, and guava are just a few examples of the tropical fruits that can add a burst of flavor to any cocktail.

Experiment with different combinations to find your perfect tropical blend.

2. Citrus Juices: Citrus fruits like lime, lemon, and orange are key to balancing the sweetness of tropical cocktails. Their tangy acidity adds a refreshing element that complements the tropical flavors beautifully.

3. Coconut: Whether it's coconut cream, coconut milk, or even coconut water, this ingredient adds a creamy and tropical touch to any cocktail. From piña coladas to coconut mojitos, coconut is a staple in many tropical concoctions.

4. Rum: No tropical cocktail would be complete without a splash of rum. With its rich and complex flavors, rum is the spirit of choice for many tropical drinks. Experiment with different types of rum, such as light, dark, or spiced, to create unique flavor profiles.

5. Herbs and Spices: Adding herbs and spices can elevate your tropical cocktails to new heights. Fresh mint, basil, ginger, and cinnamon are just a few examples of ingredients that can add depth and complexity to your creations.

6. Bitters: Bitters are a bartender's secret weapon when it comes to balancing flavors. A few drops of tropical bitters can enhance the overall taste of your cocktail and add a touch of sophistication.

7. Garnishes: Don't forget the finishing touches! From colorful umbrellas to tropical fruit slices, garnishes are an essential part of the tropical cocktail experience. They not only add visual appeal but can also enhance the aroma and flavor of the drink.

Whether you're a seasoned bartender or a home mixologist, mastering the art of tropical cocktails is a surefire way to impress your guests and transport them to a tropical paradise. So grab your shaker, gather your essential ingredients, and let your creativity flow as you embark on a flavorful journey through the world of tropical mixology. Cheers to the taste of paradise!

Piña Colada: The Tropical Vacation in a Glass

Welcome to the subchapter titled "Piña Colada: The Tropical Vacation in a Glass" from the book "Tropical Paradise: Exotic Cocktails to Transport Drinkers." In this chapter, we will explore the delightful and refreshing world of the Piña Colada, a classic tropical cocktail that embodies the essence of a vacation in every sip.

Whether you are a seasoned bartender or an enthusiastic drinker, this subchapter is perfect for anyone looking to discover new and exciting cocktails. Specifically curated for the niches of Classic Cocktails, Tropical Cocktails, Signature Cocktails, Mocktails, Whiskey Cocktails, Craft Cocktails, Gin Cocktails, Rum Cocktails, Vodka Cocktails, and Seasonal Cocktails, our aim is to provide a comprehensive guide to the Piña Colada and its variations.

The Piña Colada is a luscious blend of pineapple juice, coconut cream, and rum, creating a harmonious combination of sweet and tropical flavors. It is often garnished with a pineapple wedge and a maraschino cherry, adding a touch of visual appeal to this already enticing drink.

In this subchapter, we will not only explore the classic Piña Colada recipe but also delve into its variations, such as the Strawberry Piña Colada, Mango Piña Colada, and even the Virgin Piña Colada for those seeking a non-alcoholic option. Each variation offers a unique twist, allowing you to customize your Piña Colada experience based on your preferences and the occasion.

Furthermore, we will provide tips and tricks on how to create the perfect Piña Colada, from selecting the right ingredients to achieving the ideal consistency. Additionally, we will explore the history and origins of this tropical cocktail, taking you on a journey through its evolution and popularity over the years.

Whether you are lounging poolside, hosting a tropical-themed party, or simply craving a taste of paradise, the Piña Colada is the perfect drink to transport you to a tropical vacation in a glass. So, grab your shaker, put on some island music, and get ready to indulge in the flavors of the tropics with the Piña Colada – the ultimate tropical getaway in a glass. Cheers!

Mai Tai: A Classic Tiki Drink

In the world of tropical cocktails, there are few drinks as iconic and beloved as the Mai Tai. This classic tiki drink has become a staple in bars and lounges around the globe, transporting drinkers to a sun-soaked paradise with every sip. Whether you're a fan of classic cocktails, tropical concoctions, or signature drinks, the Mai Tai is sure to satisfy your thirst for a taste of the exotic.

The Mai Tai originated in the 1940s, created by the legendary bartender Victor J. Bergeron, better known as Trader Vic. Inspired by his travels in the South Pacific, Bergeron combined the flavors of aged rum, lime juice, orange curaçao, orgeat syrup, and a splash of grenadine to create a drink that captured the essence of the tropics. The result was a cocktail that perfectly balanced sweetness, acidity, and a hint of nuttiness.

One of the secrets to a great Mai Tai is the quality of the rum used. Traditionally, a blend of aged Jamaican and Martinique rums is recommended, as they lend depth and complexity to the drink. However, feel free to experiment with different rums to find your preferred flavor profile. Whether you choose a dark, aged rum or a lighter, fruity rum, the Mai Tai will still deliver a taste of paradise.

For those who prefer non-alcoholic mixed drinks, the Mai Tai can easily be adapted into a mocktail. Simply replace the rum with a combination of pineapple juice, orange juice, and a splash of grenadine. The result is a refreshing and tropical beverage that can be enjoyed by everyone, regardless of their alcohol preferences.

No matter the season or occasion, the Mai Tai can be enjoyed year-round. During the hot summer months, it's the perfect refresher to beat the heat, while in the winter, it can transport you to a sun-drenched beach. With its vibrant colors and tropical flavors, the Mai Tai is also a great choice for themed parties and holiday gatherings, adding a touch of exotic flair to any celebration.

So, whether you're a fan of classic cocktails, tropical drinks, or simply looking to expand your bartending repertoire, the Mai Tai is a must-try. Its timeless appeal and transportive qualities make it a favorite among drinkers of all kinds. So, grab your shaker, mix up a Mai Tai, and let the flavors of paradise whisk you away to a tropical escape.

Blue Hawaiian: A Refreshing Blue Delight

Welcome to the subchapter on the Blue Hawaiian cocktail—a tropical paradise in a glass. This vibrant and refreshing drink has become a favorite among drinkers, especially those who appreciate the exotic flavors of the tropics. Whether you are a seasoned bartender or an enthusiastic home mixologist, the Blue Hawaiian is a must-have addition to your repertoire.

Originating in the 1950s in Hawaii, the Blue Hawaiian embodies the essence of the islands with its mesmerizing blue color and tropical flavors. This cocktail perfectly balances the sweetness of pineapple juice with the tanginess of lime and the smoothness of coconut cream. The addition of rum adds a delightful kick, making it a true tropical indulgence.

For those who prefer non-alcoholic options, fear not! The Blue Hawaiian can easily be transformed into a mocktail by simply omitting the rum. The vibrant blue color and tropical flavors still make it a show-stopping drink that will transport you to a sunny beach, even without the alcohol.

In our subchapter on Tropical Cocktails: A Bartender's Guide, we explore the versatility of the Blue Hawaiian. We provide variations on the classic recipe, such as adding a splash of blue curaçao for an even more vibrant blue hue or experimenting with different types of rum to enhance the flavor profile. We also offer suggestions for garnishes, such as pineapple wedges, maraschino cherries, or even tiny cocktail umbrellas to add a touch of whimsy and fun.

The Blue Hawaiian is not limited to a specific season or occasion. In our subchapter on Seasonal Cocktails: A Bartender's Guide, we showcase how this delightful drink can be adapted to different holidays and seasons. From adding cranberry juice for a festive twist during the winter holidays to incorporating fresh berries for a refreshing summer version, the Blue Hawaiian can be enjoyed year-round.

Whether you are a fan of classic cocktails, tropical delights, or signature creations, the Blue Hawaiian has something to offer. Its vibrant blue color, tropical flavors, and refreshing taste make it a crowd-pleaser at any gathering. So grab your shaker, put on some island music, and transport yourself to a tropical paradise with the Blue Hawaiian. Cheers!

Zombie: A Potent Rum Cocktail

If you're a fan of exotic and powerful cocktails, then the Zombie is a must-try. This legendary concoction is not for the faint of heart, as it packs a serious punch. A favorite among drinkers who enjoy tropical and rum-based drinks, the Zombie will transport you to a blissful state of mind with just one sip.

Originating in the 1930s, the Zombie was created by the famous bartender Donn Beach. It quickly gained popularity and became a staple in tiki bars around the world. The name itself is a testament to its potency, as one too many of these cocktails can leave you feeling like the walking dead the next day.

The key ingredient in a Zombie is, of course, rum. This cocktail typically calls for a mixture of different types of rum, including light, dark, and overproof. The combination of these rums creates a complex flavor profile that is both sweet and tangy. To balance out the rum, fresh citrus juices like lime and grapefruit are added, along with a touch of sweetness from grenadine or other fruit syrups.

One of the defining characteristics of the Zombie is its high alcohol content. It's not uncommon for a Zombie to contain three or more shots of rum, making it one of the strongest cocktails out there. Because of this, it's important to enjoy this drink responsibly and savor it slowly.

The Zombie is a favorite among bartenders who specialize in various cocktail niches, including classic, tropical, and signature cocktails. Its bold flavors and unique combination of ingredients make it a standout choice for those looking to expand their cocktail repertoire.

Whether you're a fan of rum cocktails, looking to try something new, or simply want to indulge in a tropical paradise in a glass, the Zombie is the perfect choice. Just be warned, a few sips of this potent concoction and you'll be transported to a state of pure bliss. Cheers to the Zombie!

Hurricane: A Tropical Storm in a Glass

In the world of exotic cocktails, there is one drink that stands out like a raging storm: the Hurricane. This vibrant and flavorful concoction is a true tropical paradise in a glass, transporting drinkers to sun-soaked beaches and palm tree-lined shores. Whether you're a fan of classic cocktails, tropical flavors, signature mixes, or even non-alcoholic mocktails, the Hurricane is a must-try for every bartender and cocktail enthusiast.

Originating in the vibrant city of New Orleans, the Hurricane was born out of necessity during World War II when whiskey was in short supply. Bartenders at the famous Pat O'Brien's Bar ingeniously combined rum, passion fruit syrup, and citrus juices to create a drink that was as powerful and intense as the storm it was named after. Since then, the Hurricane has become a beloved staple in bars worldwide.

The key to a perfect Hurricane lies in the balance of flavors. The base of the cocktail is typically a blend of light and dark rum, which provides a rich and complex taste. To this, add a generous amount of passion fruit syrup, which infuses the drink with its distinctive tropical sweetness. Finally, a blend of orange and lime juices adds a refreshing citrus twist, perfectly complementing the other flavors.

For those looking to explore variations of this classic cocktail, there are endless possibilities. A whiskey-based Hurricane adds a smoky depth to the drink, while a gin-based version brings a botanical twist. Vodka lovers can also enjoy their own spin on this tropical storm by substituting rum for their favorite clear spirit.

As the seasons change, so can the Hurricane. Embrace the spirit of different holidays and occasions by incorporating seasonal ingredients. Swap out the traditional passion fruit syrup for cranberry or apple in the fall, or add a splash of sparkling wine for a festive twist during the winter holidays. The Hurricane is a versatile drink that can adapt to any celebration.

Whether you're sipping a Hurricane on a summer beach getaway or enjoying a seasonal variation during the holidays, this tropical storm in a glass is sure to transport you to a lush and exotic paradise. So raise your glass and let the Hurricane whisk you away on a gust of flavor and imagination. Cheers to the ultimate tropical cocktail experience!

Bahama Mama: A Tropical Fruit Explosion

Welcome to the subchapter titled "Bahama Mama: A Tropical Fruit Explosion" from the book "Tropical Paradise: Exotic Cocktails to Transport Drinkers." This chapter is dedicated to all the "drinkers" who love exploring new flavors and experiencing the essence of tropical paradise in their cocktails. Whether you are a fan of classic cocktails, tropical delights, signature creations, or even non-alcoholic mocktails, this subchapter will surely pique your interest.

The Bahama Mama is a legendary cocktail that embodies the vibrant colors and flavors of the Caribbean. This delightful concoction combines a medley of tropical fruits and spirits, creating a truly explosive taste experience. It is a perfect choice for those seeking a refreshing, fruity, and exotic beverage to transport them to sun-soaked beaches and swaying palm trees.

In this subchapter, we will take you on a journey through the various renditions of the Bahama Mama tailored to suit different preferences and occasions. For the classic cocktail enthusiasts, we will explore the original recipe that has stood the test of time, featuring rum, pineapple juice, coconut rum, and a hint of grenadine. The combination of sweet and tangy flavors will surely tantalize your taste buds.

If you are a fan of tropical cocktails, we will introduce you to exciting variations of the Bahama Mama. From adding fresh mango or passion fruit puree to incorporating a touch of lime or ginger, these innovative twists will elevate your drinking experience to new heights.

For those who prefer non-alcoholic options, we haven't forgotten you. We will present a mocktail version of the Bahama Mama, using a blend of tropical fruit juices and garnished with colorful fruit skewers. This refreshing and alcohol-free option will allow everyone to enjoy the tropical paradise vibes.

Whether you are a whiskey, gin, vodka, or rum lover, we will provide recommendations on how to personalize your Bahama Mama by incorporating your preferred spirit. Additionally, we will share seasonal variations of the cocktail, featuring ingredients that are perfect for different seasons and holidays, ensuring that you can enjoy a Bahama Mama all year round.

So, join us on this tropical fruit explosion journey and let the Bahama Mama whisk you away to a sun-soaked paradise with every sip. Cheers to a taste of the tropics!

Singapore Sling: A Taste of the Orient

Welcome to the subchapter on the Singapore Sling: A Taste of the Orient, where we take you on a journey to the vibrant city-state of Singapore through its iconic cocktail. Known for its unique blend of flavors and captivating history, the Singapore Sling is a must-try for any adventurous drinker.

Originating in the early 20th century at the renowned Long Bar in the Raffles Hotel, the Singapore Sling has become a classic cocktail that embodies the spirit of the Orient. This refreshing and complex drink was created by bartender Ngiam Tong Boon, who sought to craft a cocktail that would appeal to the sophisticated palates of his international clientele.

The Singapore Sling combines the sweetness of cherry liqueur with the tangy citrus flavors of lime and pineapple juice, creating a harmonious balance that is both refreshing and indulgent. To add depth and complexity, a splash of herbal liqueur, such as Benedictine or Cointreau, is added, along with a dash of grenadine for a touch of sweetness. The finishing touch is a float of aromatic bitters, which adds a subtle yet distinctive twist to the cocktail.

This tropical delight is best enjoyed in the company of friends, as it transports you to the bustling streets of Singapore. Picture yourself lounging at a rooftop bar, overlooking the city skyline, as you sip on this exquisite creation. The Singapore Sling captures the essence of the Orient, with its vibrant colors, intricate flavors, and intoxicating aroma.

Whether you are a fan of classic cocktails, tropical delights, or signature creations, the Singapore Sling is a versatile drink that caters to all tastes. It can be enjoyed as a refreshing option during the summer months or as a festive addition to your holiday celebrations. For those seeking a non-alcoholic alternative, fear not, as the Singapore Sling can easily be adapted into a mocktail by omitting the alcohol and substituting it with sparkling water or soda.

So, whether you are a seasoned drinker or a budding mixologist, the Singapore Sling is a cocktail that simply cannot be missed. With its exotic flavors and rich history, it is a testament to the art of cocktail craftsmanship. So go ahead, embark on a sensory journey, and indulge in a taste of the Orient with the Singapore Sling. Cheers!

Jungle Bird: A Tropical Rum and Campari Fusion

Welcome to the subchapter on the Jungle Bird cocktail, a delightful tropical fusion of rum and Campari. This exotic concoction is sure to transport you to a lush tropical paradise with just one sip. Whether you're a seasoned bartender or a cocktail enthusiast, this recipe is a must-try for anyone looking to explore the world of tropical cocktails.

The Jungle Bird cocktail is a unique blend of Jamaican rum, Campari, lime juice, simple syrup, and pineapple juice. The combination of these ingredients creates a harmonious balance of sweetness, bitterness, and tropical flavors that will tantalize your taste buds.

To prepare this refreshing libation, start by filling a cocktail shaker with ice. Add 1 ½ ounces of Jamaican rum, ¾ ounce of Campari, ½ ounce of lime juice, ½ ounce of simple syrup, and 1 ½ ounces of pineapple juice. Shake vigorously for about 15 seconds to ensure all the flavors are well combined.

Once you've shaken the cocktail, strain it into a chilled glass filled with ice. Garnish with a pineapple wedge and a sprig of mint to enhance the tropical presentation. The vibrant colors and aromatic garnishes will make this drink a feast for the eyes as well as the palate.

The Jungle Bird cocktail is a perfect addition to any occasion, whether you're hosting a summer pool party, enjoying a cozy night by the fireplace, or celebrating a special holiday. Its versatility allows you to enjoy it year-round, making it a staple in any bartender's repertoire.

For those looking for a non-alcoholic alternative, you can easily transform this tropical delight into a mocktail by omitting the rum and Campari. Simply replace them with a splash of soda water or a non-alcoholic spirit, and you'll have a refreshing and flavorful mocktail that everyone can enjoy.

So, whether you're a fan of classic cocktails, tropical libations, or seasonal drinks, the Jungle Bird cocktail is a must-try. Its tropical flavors, vibrant presentation, and versatility make it a favorite among bartenders and cocktail enthusiasts alike. So go ahead, shake up a Jungle Bird and let its tropical magic transport you to a blissful paradise. Cheers!

Painkiller: A Tropical Escape

Welcome to the subchapter dedicated to the Painkiller cocktail, a tropical escape in a glass. This exotic cocktail is sure to transport you to a sun-kissed beach and make you feel like you're sipping on paradise itself.

The Painkiller cocktail is a delightful blend of rum, pineapple juice, orange juice, and cream of coconut. It originated in the British Virgin Islands and has since become a favorite among beachgoers and cocktail enthusiasts alike. Its smooth and creamy texture combined with the tropical flavors make it a perfect choice for those looking to indulge in a taste of the tropics.

For the lovers of classic cocktails, the Painkiller offers a refreshing twist on the traditional rum-based drinks. It combines the richness of rum with the sweetness of pineapple and orange, creating a harmonious balance of flavors that will leave you craving for more.

If you're a fan of tropical cocktails, the Painkiller is a must-try. Its combination of pineapple and orange juices will instantly transport you to a beachside paradise, where you can kick back and relax while savoring every sip. The cream of coconut adds a creamy and velvety texture, reminiscent of a tropical vacation.

For those who prefer signature cocktails, the Painkiller is a versatile choice. It can be customized to suit your taste preferences by adjusting the amount of rum or adding a splash of grenadine for a touch of sweetness. Feel free to experiment and make it your own.

And for our non-alcoholic drinkers, the Painkiller can be easily transformed into a mocktail by simply omitting the rum. You can still enjoy the tropical flavors and indulge in a taste of the islands without the alcohol content.

No matter what your preferred spirit is, whether it's whiskey, gin, vodka, or rum, the Painkiller can be adapted to suit your taste. It's a versatile cocktail that can be enjoyed year-round, making it a perfect addition to any bartender's repertoire.

So, sit back, close your eyes, and imagine yourself on a white sandy beach with crystal clear waters. Take a sip of the Painkiller and let its tropical flavors transport you to a blissful state of relaxation. Cheers to an exotic escape in every glass!

Zombie Punch: A Festive Party Drink

Welcome to the world of Zombie Punch, the ultimate party drink that will transport you to a tropical paradise. Whether you're a fan of classic cocktails, tropical flavors, or signature creations, this drink is an absolute must-have in your bartender's guide. Not only is it perfect for drinkers, but it also caters to those seeking non-alcoholic options with its delicious mocktail version.

The Zombie Punch is a true crowd-pleaser, blending the best of both worlds: a delightful combination of rum, fruit juices, and a secret ingredient that adds a mysterious twist. As you take your first sip, you'll be instantly transported to an island paradise, surrounded by swaying palm trees and the sound of crashing waves.

For those who love the classics, the Zombie Punch offers an exciting twist on traditional cocktails. Its unique blend of rum and tropical flavors provides a refreshing take on the old favorites, making it a must-try for any bartender. Whether you're a seasoned mixologist or just starting your journey, this drink will surely impress your guests and keep them coming back for more.

If you're a fan of seasonal cocktails, Zombie Punch has you covered. With its vibrant colors and fruity flavors, this drink is a perfect fit for any occasion, whether it's a summer beach party or a Halloween-themed bash. You can even experiment with different garnishes and decorations to match the holiday spirit and create a visual masterpiece that will leave everyone in awe.

And let's not forget about the mocktail version of Zombie Punch. This non-alcoholic mixed drink is perfect for those who prefer to skip the spirits but still want to indulge in the tropical flavors. With its refreshing blend of fruit juices and a touch of sweetness, it's a fantastic option for designated drivers or anyone looking to enjoy a flavorful mocktail.

So, whether you're a fan of classic cocktails, tropical flavors, or simply looking for a delightful party drink, Zombie Punch should definitely be on your radar. Its versatility and ability to cater to different tastes make it a must-have in any bartender's guide. So go ahead, grab your shaker, and transport yourself to a tropical paradise with Zombie Punch. Cheers!

Chapter 3: Signature Cocktails: A Bartender's Guide

Creating Your Own Signature Cocktails

Are you tired of ordering the same old cocktail every time you go out? Do you want to impress your friends with a unique and personalized drink? Look no further! In this subchapter, we will guide you through the exciting process of creating your own signature cocktails.

Whether you are a lover of classic cocktails, tropical concoctions, or whiskey-based drinks, the art of crafting your own signature cocktail is a skill that every bartender should master. By experimenting with different ingredients, flavors, and techniques, you can create a drink that perfectly suits your taste and style.

To start, let's talk about the basics. Every great cocktail begins with a strong foundation of spirits. Whether you prefer gin, rum, vodka, or whiskey, choose a base spirit that you enjoy and feel comfortable working with. This will serve as the backbone of your signature creation.

Next, it's time to get creative with flavors. Consider the season or occasion you want to celebrate. For example, if you are looking to create a refreshing summer cocktail, opt for tropical fruits like pineapple, mango, or passionfruit. If you want to capture the cozy essence of winter, experiment with warm spices like cinnamon, nutmeg, or cloves.

Don't be afraid to think outside the box! Mix and match flavors that you wouldn't typically find in a cocktail. Infuse your drink with herbs, experiment with different types of bitters, or add a touch of sweetness with flavored syrups or liqueurs. The possibilities are endless!

Once you have settled on a combination of flavors, it's time to perfect the presentation. Remember, people eat and drink with their eyes first. Garnish your signature cocktail with fresh fruits, herbs, or even edible flowers. Consider using unique glassware or adding a special touch with decorative straws or cocktail umbrellas.

Lastly, don't forget to give your creation a name. A catchy and memorable name will make your signature cocktail even more special and appealing to others. Let your imagination run wild and come up with a name that reflects the essence of your drink.

In conclusion, creating your own signature cocktail is a fun and rewarding endeavor. Whether you are a seasoned bartender or an amateur mixologist, experimenting with flavors and techniques will allow you to craft a drink that is truly unique to you. So go ahead, grab your shaker, and let your creativity flow! Cheers to your very own signature cocktail!

Essential Tips for Developing Unique Cocktails

Creating unique cocktails is an art form that allows bartenders to showcase their creativity and inventiveness. Whether you're a seasoned mixologist or an aspiring bartender, mastering the skill of developing unique cocktails can set you apart in the industry. In this subchapter, we will explore essential tips that will help you craft exotic and memorable drinks that transport drinkers to a tropical paradise.

1. Understand the Basics:

Before diving into creating unique cocktails, it's crucial to have a strong foundation in classic cocktail recipes and techniques. Familiarize yourself with the classics from various niches, such as classic, tropical, whiskey, gin, rum, vodka, and craft cocktails. This knowledge will serve as a solid base for your creative experiments.

2. Experiment with Ingredients:

To develop unique cocktails, you need to be open to experimenting with different ingredients. Tropical fruits, herbs, spices, and exotic liqueurs can add depth and complexity to your drinks. Don't be afraid to mix unexpected flavor combinations and explore local ingredients to create a sense of place and uniqueness.

3. Balance is Key:

While experimenting, it's crucial to maintain a sense of balance in your cocktails. Strive for a harmony of flavors, ensuring that no single ingredient overpowers the others. Use the principles of sweet, sour, bitter, and umami to create a well-rounded and enjoyable drinking experience.

4. Presentation Matters:

The visual appeal of a cocktail can greatly enhance the overall experience. Pay attention to the glassware, garnishes, and presentation techniques you use. Experiment with different techniques like layering, muddling, and flaming to create visually stunning cocktails that leave a lasting impression.

5. Consider Seasonality:

To cater to the diverse tastes and preferences of your audience, it's important to develop seasonal cocktails. Incorporate flavors and ingredients that are associated with different seasons and holidays. This will not only keep your menu fresh and exciting but also allow you to tap into the market demand for seasonal drinks.

6. Seek Inspiration:

Developing unique cocktails requires continuous learning and inspiration. Stay updated with the latest trends in mixology, attend industry events, and join online communities to connect with other bartenders. Experiment with new techniques, explore different cultures, and draw inspiration from art, literature, and nature.

Developing unique cocktails is an ongoing journey that requires passion, creativity, and dedication. By following these essential tips, you will be well on your way to crafting exotic and unforgettable drinks that transport drinkers to a tropical paradise. So, raise your glass and embark on the exciting adventure of mixology, where the possibilities are endless.

The Art of Balancing Flavors in Signature Cocktails

In the world of mixology, creating the perfect cocktail is not just about combining different spirits and ingredients; it's about achieving a harmonious balance of flavors that tantalize the taste buds and transport drinkers to a tropical paradise. This subchapter delves into the art of balancing flavors in signature cocktails, providing invaluable insights for both novice and seasoned bartenders.

Whether you're a fan of classic cocktails, tropical delights, or whiskey-based drinks, understanding the principles of flavor balance is essential. A well-balanced cocktail should have a harmonious blend of sweet, sour, bitter, and sometimes salty or umami elements. Achieving this balance requires experimentation, skill, and a deep understanding of the individual ingredients.

For classic cocktails, such as the Old Fashioned or Martini, the focus is often on highlighting the spirit's character while adding subtle nuances. Balancing the sweetness of the sugar or simple syrup with the bitterness of the bitters and the acidity of citrus is key. A touch of salt or a savory element can elevate these drinks to new heights, enhancing the overall flavor profile.

In tropical cocktails, like the Mai Tai or Piña Colada, the emphasis is on creating a refreshing and fruity experience. Balancing the sweetness of tropical fruits with tart citrus juices and the depth of rum creates a symphony of flavors that transport drinkers to a sun-kissed beach. Experimenting with different ratios and variations of ingredients can lead to unique and signature tropical concoctions.

Signature cocktails offer bartenders the opportunity to showcase their creativity and craft. It's in these drinks that flavor balance becomes even more crucial. By carefully selecting complementary ingredients and experimenting with different proportions, bartenders can create memorable and distinctive cocktails that leave a lasting impression on the palate.

For those seeking non-alcoholic options, mocktails offer a chance to explore flavor balance without the addition of spirits. By combining fruit juices, syrups, and other non-alcoholic ingredients, bartenders can create refreshing and complex drinks that are just as enjoyable as their alcoholic counterparts.

No matter the spirit of choice – be it whiskey, gin, rum, or vodka – understanding how different flavors interact is essential for crafting exceptional cocktails. By mastering the art of balancing flavors, bartenders can create drinks that cater to different seasons and holidays, utilizing seasonal fruits, spices, and herbs to create a harmonious blend that captures the essence of the occasion.

In conclusion, the art of balancing flavors in signature cocktails is a fundamental skill that every bartender should cultivate. Whether you're crafting classic, tropical, whiskey-based, or seasonal cocktails, understanding the interplay of sweet, sour, bitter, and other flavor elements is crucial for creating memorable and delightful drinking experiences. So, grab your shaker, experiment with different ingredients, and let your creativity soar as you create your own tropical paradise in a glass. Cheers!

Signature Martini Variations

In the world of mixology, the martini is an iconic cocktail that has stood the test of time. Known for its elegance and sophistication, the martini has become synonymous with the classic cocktail culture. However, bartenders and mixologists around the world have taken this timeless drink and put their own unique spin on it. In this subchapter, we explore the world of signature martini variations that will transport you to a tropical paradise.

For those who appreciate the classics, we have the Tropical Martini. This variation takes the traditional martini and infuses it with exotic flavors like pineapple, coconut, and passion fruit. Served with a garnish of fresh tropical fruits, this martini is the perfect balance of familiar and exotic.

If you're in the mood for something a little more adventurous, try the Spicy Mango Martini. Made with fresh mango puree, lime juice, and a kick of jalapeno-infused vodka, this martini is a bold and flavorful twist on the traditional. It's the perfect drink for those who like a little heat with their sweet.

For those who prefer their cocktails on the sweeter side, the Strawberry Basil Martini is a must-try. Made with muddled strawberries, basil-infused vodka, and a hint of lime juice, this martini is a refreshing and fruity delight. The combination of fresh strawberries and fragrant basil creates a harmonious blend of flavors that will transport you straight to a tropical paradise.

If you're looking for a non-alcoholic option, the Mocktail Martini is the perfect choice. Made with a blend of fresh fruit juices, soda water, and a splash of grenadine, this mocktail captures all the flavors of a classic martini without the alcohol. It's a refreshing and vibrant drink that can be enjoyed by all.

No matter what your cocktail preference may be, there is a signature martini variation for everyone. From classic flavors to exotic twists, these variations will transport you to a tropical paradise with every sip. So grab your shaker, put on some island music, and get ready to embark on a cocktail journey like no other. Cheers to the art of mixology and the endless possibilities of the martini!

Whiskey Sour: A Personalized Twist

In the world of classic cocktails, the Whiskey Sour holds a special place. It's a timeless drink that has captivated drinkers for generations, and it's no wonder why. The combination of smooth whiskey, tangy lemon juice, and a touch of sweetness creates a flavor profile that is both refreshing and comforting. But what if we told you that you could take this beloved cocktail to new heights by adding a personalized twist?

Welcome to the world of personalized Whiskey Sours. This subchapter is dedicated to those who want to put their own spin on a classic. Whether you're a seasoned bartender or a home mixologist, this guide will inspire you to experiment and create a Whiskey Sour that is truly unique to your taste.

For those who love tropical flavors, consider adding a splash of pineapple juice or muddled mango to your Whiskey Sour. This tropical twist will transport you to a faraway beach, with the smooth whiskey acting as the perfect companion to the vibrant fruit flavors. It's a taste of paradise in a glass.

If you're a fan of craft cocktails, why not infuse your Whiskey Sour with some homemade rosemary syrup or lavender bitters? These fragrant additions will add depth and complexity to your drink, elevating it from ordinary to extraordinary. Craft cocktails are all about pushing boundaries and exploring new flavors, and a personalized Whiskey Sour is the perfect canvas for your creativity.

For the gin enthusiasts, try substituting the whiskey with a high-quality gin. The botanical notes of the gin will add a fresh and herbaceous twist to the classic recipe. It's a delightful variation that will surprise and delight your taste buds.

No matter the season or occasion, there's always a way to personalize your Whiskey Sour. From warming spices like cinnamon and nutmeg for cozy winter nights to refreshing fruits like watermelon and cucumber for hot summer days, the possibilities are endless. With a little imagination and experimentation, you can create a Whiskey Sour that perfectly captures the essence of any season or holiday.

So, grab your shaker and get ready to embark on a flavorful journey. The Whiskey Sour: A Personalized Twist subchapter is your go-to guide for creating a cocktail that is as unique as you are. Cheers to the endless possibilities and happy mixing!

Tropical Sunset: A Signature Rum and Fruit Blend

In the world of exotic cocktails, few drinks evoke the spirit of a tropical paradise quite like the Tropical Sunset. This signature rum and fruit blend is a must-try for any discerning drinker looking to be transported to a beachside oasis. Whether you're a fan of classic cocktails, tropical delights, or seeking a unique and refreshing experience, the Tropical Sunset has something to offer.

The foundation of this delightful concoction lies in the rich and flavorful world of rum. Known for its versatility and ability to transport the drinker to far-off destinations, rum is the perfect base for a tropical cocktail. The Tropical Sunset takes this beloved spirit and elevates it with a blend of tropical fruits, creating a harmonious balance of flavors that will tantalize your taste buds.

Picture yourself lounging on a white sandy beach as the sun dips below the horizon, casting a warm glow across the sky. The Tropical Sunset captures this magical moment in a glass, with its vibrant orange hues reminiscent of the setting sun. Sip by sip, you'll be transported to a tropical paradise, where worries melt away and relaxation takes over.

For those who prefer non-alcoholic options, fear not! The Tropical Sunset can easily be transformed into a mocktail by simply omitting the rum. The result is a refreshing and fruity drink that can be enjoyed by all, making it the perfect choice for any occasion.

Whether you're a seasoned bartender or an enthusiastic home mixologist, the Tropical Sunset is a must-have addition to your repertoire. Its unique combination of flavors and beautiful presentation make it a crowd-pleaser at any gathering. From whiskey and gin enthusiasts to vodka and rum connoisseurs, the Tropical Sunset offers a tropical escape for every palate.

No matter the season or occasion, the Tropical Sunset is a versatile drink that can be enjoyed year-round. Its fruity flavors make it ideal for summer celebrations, while its warm undertones perfectly complement cozy winter nights. With a little creativity, you can even adapt the recipe to feature seasonal fruits, creating a customized version that captures the essence of any holiday or special event.

So, grab your shaker and prepare to be transported to a tropical paradise with the Tropical Sunset. This signature rum and fruit blend is a true gem in the world of cocktails, offering a taste of the exotic with every sip. Cheers to the good life, and may your glass always be filled with the vibrant colors of a tropical sunset.

Vodka Infusions: Customizing Vodka Cocktails

Chapter Overview:

In this subchapter, we will explore the art of vodka infusions and how they can be used to create customized and unique vodka cocktails. From classic cocktails to tropical delights, vodka is a versatile spirit that can be easily transformed with the addition of various flavors. Whether you prefer the smoothness of a classic martini or the vibrant taste of a tropical concoction, infusing vodka allows you to elevate your drinking experience and transport yourself to a tropical paradise. This chapter is a must-read for cocktail enthusiasts who are looking to experiment with their favorite spirit.

Content:

1. Introduction to Vodka Infusions:

- Briefly explain what vodka infusions are and their popularity in the cocktail world.

- Discuss the benefits of infusing vodka, such as adding unique flavors and personalizing cocktails.

2. Infusion Techniques:

- Provide step-by-step instructions on how to infuse vodka with different ingredients, such as fruits, herbs, spices, and even flowers.

- Highlight the importance of selecting high-quality ingredients and proper infusion times.

3. Classic Vodka Cocktails with a Twist:

- Explore how infused vodka can enhance classic cocktails like the Martini, Cosmopolitan, and Bloody Mary.

- Share some popular infusion ideas that complement these timeless recipes.

4. Tropical Vodka Cocktails:

- Dive into the world of tropical flavors and showcase how infused vodka can create exotic drinks like the Mango-Pineapple Mojito or the Passionfruit Punch.

- Provide infusion suggestions that pair well with tropical fruits and ingredients.

5. Signature Vodka Cocktails:

- Encourage readers to get creative and develop their own signature vodka cocktails using infused spirits.

- Share a few unique recipes to inspire readers to experiment with their favorite flavors.

6. Seasonal Vodka Cocktails:

- Discuss how vodka infusions can be tailored to different seasons and holidays.

- Provide examples of seasonal cocktails that can be created using infused vodka, such as a Spiced Apple Martini for fall or a Cranberry-Lime Spritz for summer.

Conclusion:

Vodka infusions offer endless possibilities for customizing cocktails and elevating your drinking experience. Whether you're a fan of classic, tropical, or seasonal cocktails, this subchapter has provided you with the knowledge and inspiration to experiment with infused vodka. So grab your favorite ingredients and embark on a journey to create your very own tropical paradise in a glass. Cheers!

Gin Fizz: A Bubbly and Customizable Cocktail

When it comes to classic cocktails, few are as refreshing and versatile as the Gin Fizz. This bubbly concoction has been a favorite among drinkers for decades, and for good reason. With its light and effervescent nature, it's the perfect drink for a tropical paradise or any occasion that calls for a little extra sparkle.

The beauty of the Gin Fizz lies in its simplicity and endless customization options. The basic recipe calls for gin, lemon juice, sugar, and soda water, but you can easily elevate it to suit your taste preferences. Whether you prefer a sweeter or tart flavor profile, there are countless variations to explore.

For those who enjoy a sweeter twist, try adding a splash of fruit liqueur like raspberry or peach. This will not only enhance the flavor but also give your drink a vibrant and fruity hue. If you're in the mood for something a bit tangier, a few drops of bitters can do the trick. The addition of bitters adds complexity and depth to the cocktail, making it a perfect choice for those who enjoy a more robust taste.

Another way to customize your Gin Fizz is by experimenting with different garnishes. A classic garnish is a lemon twist, which adds a touch of citrus aroma to each sip. However, you can also get creative with herbs like rosemary or basil, or even try adding a few berries for a burst of color and flavor.

For those who prefer a non-alcoholic option, the Gin Fizz can easily be transformed into a mocktail. Simply replace the gin with a non-alcoholic alternative, such as Seedlip or a juniper-flavored tonic water. You'll still get the refreshing fizz and customizable options without the alcohol content.

No matter the season or occasion, the Gin Fizz is a versatile cocktail that can be enjoyed by all. From its bubbly nature to its customizable options, it's no wonder this drink has stood the test of time. So grab your shaker and get ready to transport yourself to a tropical paradise with a Gin Fizz in hand. Cheers!

Raspberry Mule: A Signature Vodka and Berry Mix

One of the most delightful and refreshing cocktails in the world of mixology is the Raspberry Mule. This signature drink combines the crispness of vodka with the sweetness of fresh berries, creating a perfect balance of flavors that will transport you to a tropical paradise.

For those who love classic cocktails, the Raspberry Mule is a must-try. It takes the traditional Moscow Mule and adds a fruity twist that elevates the drink to a whole new level. The combination of vodka, lime juice, and ginger beer is enhanced with the addition of muddled raspberries. The result is a vibrant and tangy concoction that will tantalize your taste buds and leave you craving for more.

If you are a lover of tropical cocktails, the Raspberry Mule is a drink that should be at the top of your list. The burst of berry flavors, coupled with the zing of lime and the spiciness of ginger, will transport you to a sunny beach, with the gentle ocean breeze caressing your face. Whether you are sipping this delightful concoction by the poolside or enjoying a beach picnic, the Raspberry Mule is the ultimate tropical escape in a glass.

For those seeking a signature cocktail that will impress their guests, look no further than the Raspberry Mule. Its vibrant pink hue and garnish of fresh raspberries make it visually stunning, while the complex flavors will leave your guests in awe. Whether you are hosting a summer soirée or a cocktail party, this drink is sure to be a crowd-pleaser.

For those who prefer non-alcoholic mixed drinks, the Raspberry Mule can easily be transformed into a refreshing mocktail. Simply replace the vodka with sparkling water or ginger ale, and you will have a delicious and alcohol-free version that is just as enjoyable.

No matter what your preferred liquor of choice is, the Raspberry Mule can be adapted to suit your taste. Swap out the vodka for whiskey, gin, rum, or even craft spirits, and you will have a unique variation that will cater to your preferences.

Whether you are sipping a Raspberry Mule on a warm summer day, enjoying it as a festive seasonal cocktail, or experimenting with different liquor combinations, this drink is a true gem in the world of mixology. So grab your shaker, muddle some raspberries, and transport yourself to a tropical paradise with this signature vodka and berry mix.

Spiced Old Fashioned: A Unique Whiskey Creation

In the realm of classic cocktails, few are as timeless and revered as the Old Fashioned. This iconic drink has stood the test of time, captivating drinkers with its simplicity and elegance. However, in the spirit of innovation and experimentation, mixologists have taken the Old Fashioned to new heights by infusing it with exotic spices, resulting in a truly unique concoction – the Spiced Old Fashioned.

Crafted with a careful selection of premium whiskey, the Spiced Old Fashioned remains true to its roots while offering a tantalizing twist of flavors. The addition of aromatic spices such as cinnamon, cloves, and nutmeg adds a warm and inviting complexity to the drink, elevating it to a whole new level of indulgence. With each sip, drinkers are transported to a tropical paradise, where the air is filled with the enticing aromas of distant lands.

The Spiced Old Fashioned is the embodiment of the fusion between classic and tropical cocktails. It is a testament to the versatility of whiskey, showcasing its ability to adapt to different flavor profiles and create a harmonious balance. Whether you are a fan of classic cocktails, tropical libations, or both, this drink is sure to captivate your taste buds and transport you to a world of exotic flavors.

For those who prefer non-alcoholic options, fear not! The Spiced Old Fashioned can easily be transformed into a mocktail by substituting the whiskey with a high-quality alcohol-free alternative. The spices will still shine through, offering a satisfying and refreshing beverage for those abstaining from alcohol.

As with any great cocktail, the key to a perfect Spiced Old Fashioned lies in the art of mixology. Skilled bartenders know how to balance the flavors, ensuring that each ingredient complements the others without overpowering the delicate nuances of the whiskey. It is a drink that requires patience, precision, and a deep understanding of the craft.

Whether you are a whiskey aficionado, a lover of tropical flavors, or simply someone seeking a unique and unforgettable drinking experience, the Spiced Old Fashioned is a must-try. It is a cocktail that transcends boundaries, appealing to the classic, tropical, and seasonal cocktail enthusiasts alike. So, sit back, relax, and let this captivating creation transport you to a tropical paradise with every sip.

Margarita Remix: Putting a Twist on a Classic

As a bartender, it's always exciting to experiment and put a unique spin on classic cocktails. One such drink that has stood the test of time and continues to be a favorite among drinkers is the Margarita. Originating in Mexico, this refreshing blend of tequila, lime juice, and Triple Sec has become a staple in bars worldwide. In our book, "Tropical Paradise: Exotic Cocktails to Transport Drinkers," we explore how to take the Margarita to new heights by adding exciting twists that will surely transport you to a tropical paradise.

For the lovers of classic cocktails, we understand the importance of preserving the essence of the Margarita while infusing it with new flavors. One way we achieve this is by introducing tropical fruits like mango or pineapple to create a fruity Margarita that is both refreshing and exotic. Imagine sipping on a Mango Margarita, the sweetness of the fruit perfectly balanced with the tangy lime and the kick of tequila. It's a taste of paradise that will transport you to a beachside getaway.

For those looking to explore the world of craft cocktails, we delve into the art of mixology by incorporating unique ingredients and techniques to elevate the Margarita. How about a Smoky Margarita, where we infuse the tequila with a hint of mesquite or hickory smoke? The result is a complex and smoky flavor profile that adds depth to the classic Margarita. Or for the adventurous drinkers, we introduce the Spicy Margarita, where we infuse the tequila with jalapeno peppers for a fiery kick that will awaken your taste buds.

In our book, we also cater to the whiskey, gin, vodka, and rum enthusiasts by providing variations of the Margarita that feature these spirits. From a Whiskey Margarita with a smoky bourbon twist to a Gin Margarita infused with botanical flavors, we offer something for every palate.

Moreover, we understand the importance of seasonal cocktails in keeping the drinks menu exciting and relevant. Throughout the book, we showcase Margarita variations that are perfect for different seasons and holidays. From a refreshing Watermelon Margarita for summer to a Spiced Apple Margarita for fall, these seasonal twists on the classic Margarita will keep you in the festive spirit all year round.

Whether you are a fan of classic cocktails, tropical flavors, or unique craft creations, "Tropical Paradise: Exotic Cocktails to Transport Drinkers" has something for everyone. Join us on a journey to explore the Margarita like never before and let us transport you to a tropical paradise with every sip. Cheers!

Berry Mojito: A Refreshing Signature Rum Drink

In the vibrant world of tropical cocktails, the Berry Mojito stands tall as a refreshing and invigorating drink that transports you straight to a sun-soaked paradise. This delightful concoction is a perfect blend of classic flavors and exotic ingredients, making it a favorite among bartenders and cocktail enthusiasts alike.

The Berry Mojito starts with the star of the show: rum. This versatile spirit adds a smooth and rich character to the drink, elevating its taste and creating a perfect balance with the other ingredients. Whether you prefer dark, light, or flavored rum, each variant brings its own unique twist to the Berry Mojito.

To give this cocktail its signature tropical flair, fresh berries are muddled with lime juice and a touch of simple syrup. This infusion of flavors creates a burst of sweetness and tanginess that perfectly complements the rum. The addition of mint leaves adds a refreshing and herbaceous note, enhancing the overall experience of sipping this delightful beverage.

As with any cocktail, presentation is key. The Berry Mojito is traditionally served in a tall glass filled with crushed ice, allowing you to marvel at its vibrant colors and enticing aromas. Garnished with a sprig of fresh mint and a few extra berries, this drink is a visual feast that is as pleasing to the eyes as it is to the taste buds.

The versatility of the Berry Mojito makes it an ideal choice for any occasion. Whether you're sipping it poolside on a hot summer day or enjoying it at a festive holiday gathering, this drink is sure to transport you to a tropical paradise with every sip. Its refreshing nature also makes it a popular choice for those seeking a non-alcoholic option, as the recipe can easily be adapted into a mocktail by omitting the rum.

So, whether you're a classic cocktail connoisseur, a lover of all things tropical, or simply someone looking for a refreshing and flavorful drink, the Berry Mojito is a must-try. Its unique blend of rum, berries, lime, and mint will transport you to a tropical paradise, no matter where you are. Cheers to the Berry Mojito - a true signature rum drink that captures the essence of an exotic escape in every sip.

Chapter 4: Mocktails: A Bartender's Guide (non-alcoholic mixed drinks)

The Rise of Mocktails: A Trendy Alternative

In recent years, there has been a noticeable shift in the drinking habits of people all around the world. While alcoholic beverages have always been a popular choice, a new trend is emerging – the rise of mocktails. Mocktails, also known as non-alcoholic mixed drinks, have become a trendy alternative for those looking to enjoy a delicious and refreshing beverage without the effects of alcohol.

For drinkers who are seeking a healthier lifestyle or simply want to cut back on their alcohol consumption, mocktails offer a welcome solution. These alcohol-free concoctions are made using a variety of ingredients such as fresh fruits, herbs, and flavored syrups, resulting in a burst of flavors that can rival their alcoholic counterparts.

Mocktails have also found their place in the world of bartending. Bartenders are now creating elaborate and innovative mocktail recipes that cater to a wide range of tastes and preferences. From fruity and tropical mocktails that transport drinkers to a tropical paradise, to sophisticated and elegant mocktails that are perfect for special occasions, there is a mocktail for every palate.

For those who enjoy classic cocktails, tropical cocktails, signature cocktails, or any other type of cocktail, mocktails provide a unique and exciting twist. Bartenders can now showcase their creativity and mixology skills by designing mocktails that are just as visually stunning and delicious as their alcoholic counterparts.

The popularity of mocktails has also extended to specific niches within the bartending industry. Whether you are a fan of whiskey cocktails, craft cocktails, gin cocktails, rum cocktails, vodka cocktails, or seasonal cocktails, there are mocktail recipes tailored to suit your preferences. Bartender's guides dedicated to mocktails provide a wealth of inspiration and guidance for creating non-alcoholic drinks that are both impressive and satisfying.

Furthermore, mocktails are not just a passing trend. They have become a permanent fixture in bars and restaurants around the world. As more people embrace a mindful and balanced approach to drinking, mocktails offer a guilt-free option that allows everyone to partake in the joy of a well-crafted and delicious beverage.

So, whether you are looking to enjoy a night out without the effects of alcohol, exploring new flavors and taste combinations, or simply seeking a healthier alternative, the rise of mocktails provides an exciting and trendy option for drinkers of all kinds. Embrace the mocktail revolution and embark on a flavorful journey that will transport you to a tropical paradise, no matter the occasion or season.

Essential Ingredients for Mocktails

Subchapter: Essential Ingredients for Mocktails

Mocktails are becoming increasingly popular among drinkers who either prefer non-alcoholic options or want to enjoy a refreshing drink without the effects of alcohol. These alcohol-free mixed drinks offer endless possibilities for creativity and flavor combinations. To create the perfect mocktail, it is important to have a few essential ingredients on hand. Here are some must-have ingredients for your mocktail adventures.

1. Fresh Fruits: Fresh fruits are the backbone of any good mocktail. Whether it's citrus fruits like lemons and limes, or tropical fruits like pineapple and mango, they provide natural sweetness and vibrant

flavors. Experiment with different fruits to add depth and complexity to your mocktails.

2. Fruit Juices: Alongside fresh fruits, fruit juices are essential for mocktail mixology. Stock your bar with a variety of juices like orange, cranberry, grapefruit, and pomegranate. These juices not only add sweetness but also serve as a base for many mocktail recipes.

3. Syrups and Purees: To elevate the flavors of your mocktails, invest in a selection of syrups and purees. Vanilla syrup, grenadine, simple syrup, and flavored purees like strawberry or peach can add a delicious twist to your creations. These ingredients help balance the flavors and add a touch of sweetness.

4. Bitters and Tinctures: Just because a mocktail is alcohol-free doesn't mean it can't have complexity. Bitters and tinctures, available in a variety of flavors, can add depth and sophistication to your mocktail recipes. A few drops of aromatic bitters like orange or lavender can transform a simple mocktail into a refined and balanced drink.

5. Fresh Herbs and Spices: Incorporating fresh herbs and spices can take your mocktails to the next level. Mint, basil, cilantro, and rosemary can add freshness and aroma, while spices like cinnamon, ginger, and nutmeg can lend warmth and complexity. Experiment with different combinations to find your favorite flavor profiles.

6. Soda Water and Tonic Water: Carbonated elements are essential for adding a refreshing fizz to your mocktails. Stock up on soda water and tonic water to give your drinks that effervescent touch. They can also be used as mixers to add volume and balance to the mocktail.

By having these essential ingredients on hand, you'll be well-equipped to create an array of delicious mocktails that cater to various tastes and occasions. So, whether you're hosting a party, enjoying a night in, or simply looking for a refreshing alternative, these ingredients will help you craft mocktails that are bursting with flavor and creativity. Cheers to the world of mocktails!

Virgin Piña Colada: A Tropical Mocktail Delight

Welcome to the subchapter on the Virgin Piña Colada, a tropical mocktail delight that will transport you straight to a sun-drenched beach. Whether you're looking for a refreshing non-alcoholic option, or simply want to enjoy the flavors of a classic cocktail without the alcohol, the Virgin Piña Colada is the perfect choice.

For those who are unfamiliar, the Piña Colada is a popular tropical cocktail that combines the sweetness of pineapple, the creaminess of coconut, and the smoothness of rum. However, in our version, we've removed the rum and created a mocktail that is equally as delicious and satisfying.

The Virgin Piña Colada starts with the star ingredient, pineapple juice. Bursting with tropical flavor, pineapple juice forms the base of this mocktail. It's then blended with coconut cream, which adds a velvety texture and a rich, creamy taste. Together, these two ingredients create a mouthwatering combination that will transport you to a tropical paradise with every sip.

To enhance the presentation and taste, we recommend garnishing your Virgin Piña Colada with a pineapple wedge and a maraschino cherry. The bright colors and fruity accents will make you feel like you're sipping this mocktail on a secluded beach, with the sun warming your skin and the sound of waves crashing in the distance.

The Virgin Piña Colada is not only a refreshing and delicious drink, but it's also versatile. You can enjoy it as a standalone mocktail or pair it with your favorite tropical dishes. It's the perfect accompaniment to a beach picnic or a poolside gathering with friends and family.

In conclusion, the Virgin Piña Colada is a tropical mocktail delight that captures the essence of a classic cocktail without the alcohol. It's a refreshing and delicious option for those who want to indulge in the flavors of a tropical paradise while abstaining from alcohol. So sit back, relax, and let the Virgin Piña Colada transport you to a sun-soaked beach with every sip.

Cheers to the perfect tropical mocktail!

Shirley Temple: A Classic Mocktail for All Ages

In the world of cocktails, there are classics that stand the test of time, and one such timeless drink is the Shirley Temple. This delightful mocktail has been a favorite among both kids and adults for decades. It's a refreshing and vibrant drink that can transport you to a tropical paradise with just one sip.

The Shirley Temple is a non-alcoholic mixed drink that was named after the famous child actress of the 1930s, Shirley Temple. It's a simple yet elegant blend of ginger ale, grenadine syrup, and a dash of fresh lime juice. The combination of these ingredients creates a sweet and tangy flavor profile that is sure to please any palate.

What makes the Shirley Temple so special is its versatility. While it's commonly enjoyed by those who prefer non-alcoholic beverages, it can also be easily transformed into a cocktail by adding a splash of vodka or rum. This makes it a perfect choice for any occasion, whether you're hosting a family gathering, a tropical-themed party, or a casual get-together with friends.

For those who love classic cocktails, the Shirley Temple is a must-try. Its iconic status and timeless appeal have made it a staple in bars and restaurants all over the world. Bartenders often include this drink in their repertoire as it appeals to a wide range of customers, from those seeking a nostalgic experience to those looking for a refreshing and alcohol-free option.

If you're a fan of tropical cocktails, the Shirley Temple is a great choice to add to your repertoire. With its combination of ginger ale and lime juice, it brings a taste of the tropics to your glass. Sipping on a Shirley Temple can instantly transport you to a sunny beach, complete with swaying palm trees and crystal-clear waters.

Whether you're a seasoned mixologist or just starting your journey into the world of cocktails, the Shirley Temple is a drink that should not be overlooked. Its simplicity, versatility, and timeless appeal make it a favorite among drinkers of all ages. So grab your favorite glass, fill it with ice, and enjoy a refreshing Shirley Temple - a classic mocktail that never goes out of style.

Blueberry Lemonade: A Refreshing Summer Mocktail

Summer is all about sipping on cool, refreshing drinks that transport you to a tropical paradise. And what better way to beat the heat than with a delicious mocktail that combines the tangy flavors of blueberries and lemons? Introducing the Blueberry Lemonade, a mocktail that will leave you craving for more.

Perfect for those who prefer non-alcoholic beverages, the Blueberry Lemonade is a delightful blend of sweet and sour, making it a crowd-pleaser at any summer gathering. This mocktail is not only refreshing but also packed with vitamins and antioxidants, thanks to the abundance of blueberries.

To make this tantalizing mocktail, start by muddling a handful of fresh blueberries in a glass. This will release their natural juices and create a vibrant base for the drink. Next, add freshly squeezed lemon juice to provide a zesty kick that perfectly complements the sweetness of the blueberries.

For an extra touch of sweetness, a simple syrup made from sugar and water can be added to taste. However, if you prefer a healthier option, feel free to substitute the simple syrup with a natural sweetener like honey or agave nectar.

To complete this refreshing mocktail, fill the glass with ice and top it off with sparkling water or lemon-lime soda. The effervescence adds a delightful fizz to the drink, making it even more enjoyable on a hot summer day.

The Blueberry Lemonade is not only a treat for the taste buds but also a feast for the eyes. Garnish the mocktail with a sprig of fresh mint and a few extra blueberries to create a visually appealing presentation that will impress your guests.

Whether you're hosting a poolside party, a backyard barbecue, or simply lounging on your patio, the Blueberry Lemonade is the perfect summer mocktail to keep you refreshed and hydrated. So, grab a glass, take a sip, and let the flavors transport you to a tropical paradise.

This recipe is just one of many exotic mocktails featured in our book, "Tropical Paradise: Exotic Cocktails to Transport Drinkers." Whether you're a fan of classic cocktails, tropical concoctions, or signature drinks, our bartender's guide has something for everyone. From whiskey and rum cocktails to craft and gin creations, we've got you covered for every occasion.

So, why wait? Dive into the world of refreshing mocktails and tantalizing cocktails with our bartender's guide. Cheers to a summer filled with delicious drinks and unforgettable moments!

Virgin Mojito: A Minty and Citrusy Mocktail

In the world of cocktails, the Virgin Mojito stands out as a refreshing and vibrant mocktail option for those seeking a delicious non-alcoholic drink. With its combination of mint, lime, and sparkling water, this mocktail is perfect for any occasion, whether you're looking for a healthy alternative or simply want to enjoy a refreshing beverage.

The Virgin Mojito is a classic mocktail that captures the essence of a traditional Mojito without the addition of alcohol. It is a perfect choice for those who want to enjoy the flavors of a tropical cocktail without the buzz. This mocktail is also a great option for designated drivers or those who prefer not to consume alcohol.

The base of the Virgin Mojito is fresh and aromatic mint leaves. Mint adds a burst of freshness and a cooling sensation to the drink, making it perfect for hot summer days. The lime juice adds a tangy and citrusy flavor that balances the sweetness of the drink. Combined with sparkling water, the Virgin Mojito becomes a fizzy and invigorating mocktail.

To prepare a Virgin Mojito, start by muddling fresh mint leaves and lime juice in a glass. This muddling process releases the essential oils from the mint leaves, enhancing the drink's flavor and aroma. Add a touch of simple syrup, which can be adjusted according to personal preference, to sweeten the mocktail. Finally, top it off with sparkling water and garnish with a sprig of mint and a slice of lime. The result is a visually appealing and delicious mocktail that will transport you to a tropical paradise.

The Virgin Mojito is a versatile mocktail that can be customized to suit individual tastes. For those who prefer a sweeter drink, additional simple syrup can be added. Some variations even include fresh fruits like strawberries or raspberries, adding a burst of fruity goodness to the mocktail. The possibilities are endless, allowing you to experiment and create your own signature Virgin Mojito.

Whether you're a fan of classic cocktails, tropical drinks, or seasonal creations, the Virgin Mojito is a must-try mocktail for any bartender or drink enthusiast. Its minty and citrusy flavors, combined with its refreshing fizz, make it a perfect choice for any occasion. So sit back, relax, and enjoy a taste of paradise with a Virgin Mojito in hand. Cheers!

Mango Sunrise: A Tropical Non-Alcoholic Treat

Welcome to the subchapter titled "Mango Sunrise: A Tropical Non-Alcoholic Treat" from the book "Tropical Paradise: Exotic Cocktails to Transport Drinkers." In this chapter, we will explore the refreshing and vibrant world of non-alcoholic tropical beverages, specifically focusing on the delightful Mango Sunrise.

For those who prefer to enjoy a tropical drink without the buzz, Mango Sunrise is the perfect choice. Bursting with the flavors of ripe mangoes and tangy citrus, this mocktail will transport you to a sun-kissed beach, even if you're sipping it from the comfort of your own home.

To create the Mango Sunrise, you will need a few simple ingredients that can be easily found in your local grocery store or tropical fruit market. Start by gathering fresh mangoes, orange juice, grenadine syrup, and a splash of lime juice. These ingredients combine to create a vibrant and refreshing drink that will impress even the most discerning drinkers.

To make the Mango Sunrise, begin by peeling and slicing the mangoes, removing the pit. Place the mango slices in a blender and add the orange juice and lime juice. Blend until smooth and creamy, ensuring there are no chunks of fruit remaining.

Now comes the fun part – the sunrise effect. Pour the mango mixture into a tall glass, filling it about three-quarters of the way. Slowly pour in the grenadine syrup, allowing it to sink to the bottom of the glass. As it settles, it will create a beautiful gradient of colors, resembling a tropical sunrise.

Garnish your Mango Sunrise with a slice of fresh mango or a wedge of lime, and you're ready to enjoy this tropical delight. Take a sip and let the flavors transport you to a faraway beach, where the sun shines brightly and the ocean breeze caresses your skin.

Whether you're a fan of classic cocktails, tropical concoctions, or seasonal beverages, the Mango Sunrise is a must-try for any bartender or drink enthusiast. Its tropical flavors, refreshing taste, and vibrant presentation make it a versatile option for any occasion, from summer parties to holiday gatherings.

So, why not add a touch of the tropics to your drink repertoire? The Mango Sunrise is a delightful non-alcoholic treat that will transport you to a tropical paradise with every sip. Cheers to a flavorful and refreshing experience that will leave you craving more.

Cranberry Sparkler: A Festive Mocktail for Celebrations

In the world of mixology, there's always room for a dazzling mocktail that can elevate any celebration. And when it comes to creating a drink that's both refreshing and full of festive spirit, the Cranberry Sparkler takes center stage. This delightful concoction combines the tartness of cranberry juice with the effervescence of sparkling water, making it the perfect choice for those looking for a non-alcoholic option that still packs a punch.

Whether you're a seasoned bartender or a home enthusiast, this recipe is a must-have for your repertoire. It not only appeals to the Classic Cocktail lovers who appreciate timeless elegance, but also to the Tropical Cocktail enthusiasts who crave exotic flavors. The Cranberry Sparkler is versatile enough to be enjoyed year-round, making it a favorite among those who love Seasonal Cocktails tailored to different holidays and seasons.

The base of this mocktail is cranberry juice, which brings a tangy and slightly sweet taste to the mix. To add depth and complexity, a splash of fresh lime juice is added, balancing the flavors and giving it a refreshing kick. For those who enjoy a touch of sweetness, a hint of simple syrup can be added, although the natural sweetness of cranberry juice is often enough.

To truly make this drink sparkle, top it off with a generous pour of sparkling water. This effervescent touch adds a celebratory fizz and lightness to the mocktail, making it an irresistible option for any occasion. Garnish with a sprig of fresh mint or a twist of lime, and you have a visually appealing drink that's ready to impress.

The Cranberry Sparkler is perfect for those who want to indulge in a flavorful and festive mocktail without missing out on the fun. Its versatility and wide appeal make it a beloved choice for bartenders and cocktail enthusiasts alike. So, whether you're hosting a tropical-themed party, a classic cocktail soirée, or just looking for a refreshing drink to enjoy on a hot summer day, the Cranberry Sparkler is sure to transport you to a tropical paradise of flavors.

Ginger Beer Mocktail: A Spicy and Refreshing Blend

In the world of exotic cocktails, there is a drink that stands out for its unique blend of flavors and refreshing qualities: the Ginger Beer Mocktail. This non-alcoholic mixed drink combines the fiery kick of ginger with the crispness of soda, creating a beverage that is both spicy and invigorating.

Perfect for those looking to enjoy a delicious and satisfying mocktail, the Ginger Beer Mocktail is a favorite among bartenders and drinkers alike. With its vibrant combination of flavors, it appeals to a wide range of tastes and preferences, making it a versatile choice for any occasion.

The key ingredient in this mocktail is ginger beer, a non-alcoholic carbonated beverage that is made by fermenting ginger root. This gives the drink its distinctive spicy and tangy flavor, which is further enhanced by the addition of fresh lime juice. The result is a refreshing and zesty drink that is perfect for hot summer days or as a pick-me-up at any time of the year.

To make the Ginger Beer Mocktail, simply combine ginger beer, lime juice, and a dash of simple syrup in a glass filled with ice. Stir gently to blend the flavors together and garnish with a slice of lime or a sprig of fresh mint. The result is a vibrant and visually appealing drink that is as delicious to taste as it is to look at.

This mocktail is not only a hit with those seeking a non-alcoholic alternative to traditional cocktails, but it also pairs well with a variety of foods. Its spicy and refreshing qualities make it an excellent companion to spicy dishes, seafood, or even grilled meats. Its versatility makes it a must-have addition to any bartender's repertoire.

Whether you are a fan of classic cocktails, tropical concoctions, or signature drinks, the Ginger Beer Mocktail is sure to impress. Its spicy and refreshing blend of flavors will transport you to a tropical paradise with every sip. So, why not try this enticing mocktail today and experience a taste sensation like no other? Cheers to the Ginger Beer Mocktail!

Watermelon Cooler: A Refreshing Mocktail for Hot Days

When the sun is blazing and the heat is unbearable, nothing quenches your thirst quite like a cool and refreshing drink. And what better way to beat the heat than with a watermelon cooler? This mocktail is the perfect blend of sweet and tangy, making it a favorite among drinkers looking for a non-alcoholic option.

In this subchapter, we bring you the recipe for the ultimate watermelon cooler, guaranteed to transport you to a tropical paradise with every sip. Whether you're a fan of classic cocktails, tropical cocktails, or signature cocktails, this mocktail is a must-try for all drink enthusiasts.

One of the best things about this watermelon cooler is its versatility. It pairs well with various spirits, making it an excellent choice for whiskey, craft, gin, rum, and vodka cocktail lovers. You can even experiment with different seasonal variations to create a drink that suits every holiday and occasion.

To create this tantalizing mocktail, you'll need fresh watermelon, lime juice, club soda, and a touch of sweetness with simple syrup or agave nectar. The combination of juicy watermelon and zesty lime creates a burst of flavors that will leave your taste buds craving for more.

Prepare the drink by blending the watermelon chunks until smooth, and then strain the juice to remove any pulp. Add lime juice and sweetener according to your taste preferences. Fill a glass with ice, pour the watermelon mixture over it, and top it off with chilled club soda. Garnish with a sprig of mint or a slice of lime for an extra touch of freshness.

Not only is this watermelon cooler incredibly delicious, but it's also packed with health benefits. Watermelon is hydrating, rich in vitamins, and a great source of antioxidants, making it the perfect guilt-free indulgence on a hot summer day.

So, the next time you're in need of a refreshing mocktail, look no further than the watermelon cooler. With its tropical vibes and invigorating flavors, it's sure to transport you to a paradise of relaxation and enjoyment. Get ready to raise your glass and drink your way to a cool and revitalizing experience!

Virgin Margarita: A Citrusy Mocktail Twist

In the world of cocktails, the Margarita stands tall as a classic favorite. With its refreshing combination of tequila, lime juice, and orange liqueur, it has become a go-to drink for many. But what about those who prefer to skip the alcohol? Introducing the Virgin Margarita – a citrusy mocktail twist that captures all the flavors of the original without the buzz.

Whether you're a designated driver, pregnant, or simply prefer the taste of a non-alcoholic beverage, the Virgin Margarita is the perfect choice. It offers a zesty blend of fresh lime juice, orange juice, and a touch of sweetness from simple syrup. This mocktail is not only refreshing but also easy to make, allowing you to enjoy the flavors of a classic Margarita anytime, anywhere.

To craft this tantalizing mocktail, start by rimming a glass with salt, just like you would for a traditional Margarita. This adds an extra burst of flavor and a touch of elegance. Next, combine freshly squeezed lime juice, orange juice, and simple syrup in a cocktail shaker filled with ice. Shake vigorously to mix all the ingredients and strain the mocktail into the salt-rimmed glass. Garnish with a lime wedge or a slice of orange for a vibrant presentation.

The Virgin Margarita pairs well with a variety of cuisines, making it a versatile choice for any occasion. Its citrusy notes complement spicy Mexican dishes, while its refreshing profile makes it a perfect accompaniment to seafood or grilled meats. It's also a great option for those looking for a non-alcoholic alternative during festive seasons or when celebrating holidays.

Whether you're exploring classic cocktails, tropical concoctions, or seeking seasonal inspiration, the Virgin Margarita is a must-try addition to your bartender's guide. Its citrusy twist brings a burst of flavor to any occasion, making it a staple in the world of mocktails. So, raise a glass and indulge in the refreshing flavors of this citrus-infused delight – the Virgin Margarita awaits!

Sparkling Berry Punch: A Fruity Mocktail for Parties

Looking to add a touch of tropical paradise to your next party? Look no further than the Sparkling Berry Punch, a delightful fruity mocktail that will transport your taste buds to a sun-soaked beach. Whether you're a seasoned drinker or a fan of non-alcoholic mixed drinks, this refreshing mocktail is sure to be a hit.

Perfect for any occasion, the Sparkling Berry Punch is a versatile drink that can be enjoyed year-round. It's a great addition to any bartender's repertoire, whether you specialize in classic cocktails, tropical cocktails, signature cocktails, or craft cocktails. This mocktail is also a fantastic option for those who prefer whiskey, gin, rum, or vodka cocktails.

The Sparkling Berry Punch is made with a vibrant blend of berries, citrus, and sparkling water, creating a burst of flavors that will tantalize your taste buds. The recipe is simple yet elegant, making it easy to whip up a batch for your next gathering.

To make this refreshing mocktail, start by muddling a handful of fresh berries, such as raspberries and blueberries, in a cocktail shaker. Add freshly squeezed lemon and lime juice for a zesty kick, along with a touch of simple syrup for sweetness. Shake well to combine the flavors, then strain the mixture into a glass filled with ice.

Top off the mocktail with sparkling water for a fizzy finish, and garnish with a sprig of fresh mint or a wedge of lime. The result is a vibrant, flavorful drink that will impress your guests and transport them to a tropical paradise.

The Sparkling Berry Punch is also a fantastic option for seasonal cocktails, as you can easily switch up the berries depending on the time of year. Use strawberries and blackberries for a summery twist, or cranberries and pomegranate seeds for a festive holiday version.

So, whether you're hosting a summer soiree, a winter holiday party, or simply want to treat yourself to a refreshing drink, the Sparkling Berry Punch is the perfect choice. It's a fruity mocktail that will transport you to a tropical paradise with every sip. Cheers to a taste of paradise!

Chapter 5: Whiskey Cocktails: A Bartender's Guide

Introduction to Whiskey Cocktails

Whiskey is a versatile and beloved spirit that has been enjoyed by drinkers around the world for centuries. Its rich and complex flavors make it a perfect base for crafting delicious cocktails that can transport you to a tropical paradise. In this subchapter, we will explore the art of creating whiskey cocktails that will tantalize your taste buds and elevate your drinking experience.

Whether you are a seasoned whiskey connoisseur or just starting to explore the world of cocktails, this chapter is designed to cater to all levels of expertise. From classic cocktails to innovative creations, we will cover a wide range of whiskey-based drinks that will satisfy any palate.

In Classic Cocktails: A Bartender's Guide, we will delve into the timeless and iconic whiskey cocktails that have stood the test of time. From the sophisticated Old Fashioned to the refreshing Whiskey Sour, you will learn the secrets behind these beloved classics and how to make them to perfection.

For those seeking a taste of the tropics, Tropical Cocktails: A Bartender's Guide will introduce you to exotic whiskey concoctions that will transport you to a sun-soaked beach. Imagine sipping on a Pineapple Whiskey Smash or a Coconut Whiskey Punch – these vibrant and fruity drinks will instantly transport you to a tropical paradise.

Signature Cocktails: A Bartender's Guide will showcase unique and innovative whiskey cocktails created by top mixologists. These one-of-a-kind drinks are perfect for those looking to impress their guests or simply indulge in a luxurious and decadent cocktail experience.

If you prefer non-alcoholic options, Mocktails: A Bartender's Guide will offer a selection of whiskey-inspired drinks without the alcohol. These mocktails are crafted with the same attention to detail and flavor profiles as their alcoholic counterparts, ensuring that everyone can enjoy a delicious and satisfying beverage.

Whiskey Cocktails: A Bartender's Guide will take an in-depth look at the various types of whiskey available and how they can be used to create different flavor profiles in cocktails. From bourbon to scotch, rye to Irish whiskey, you will discover the unique characteristics of each and how they can be incorporated into your favorite drinks.

Craft Cocktails: A Bartender's Guide will explore the art of mixology and how to create your own signature whiskey cocktails. Learn the techniques and tools used by professional bartenders to craft unique and personalized drinks that reflect your individual taste and style.

In addition to whiskey, we will also explore other popular spirits in their respective chapters. From the smooth and aromatic world of gin cocktails to the vibrant and tropical realm of rum cocktails, there is something for everyone in this comprehensive bartender's guide.

Finally, Seasonal Cocktails: A Bartender's Guide will feature drinks that celebrate different seasons and holidays. From cozy winter warmers to refreshing summer sippers, these seasonal whiskey cocktails will help you embrace the spirit of each occasion and create unforgettable memories.

Whether you are looking to expand your cocktail repertoire, impress your guests, or simply enjoy a delicious drink, this subchapter on Introduction to Whiskey Cocktails will provide you with all the knowledge and inspiration you need to elevate your whiskey drinking experience. So grab your shaker, pour yourself a glass, and let's embark on a journey to tropical paradise through the world of whiskey cocktails. Cheers!

Essential Whiskey Types and Their Characteristics

In the world of cocktails, whiskey holds a special place. Its rich and complex flavors add depth to any drink, making it a favorite among bartenders and enthusiasts alike. If you're a whiskey lover or curious to explore this classic spirit, understanding the different types of whiskey and their unique characteristics is essential. In this subchapter, we'll delve into the world of whiskey and discover its various styles, flavors, and origins.

1. Scotch Whisky: Hailing from Scotland, Scotch whisky is known for its smoky and peaty profile. Distilled from malted barley, it is aged in oak barrels for a minimum of three years. Whether you prefer a smoky Islay or a smooth Speyside, Scotch whisky offers a wide range of flavors to suit every palate.

2. Irish Whiskey: Distinctively smooth and triple-distilled, Irish whiskey is a favorite for those seeking a lighter and more approachable option. With notes of honey, vanilla, and fruit, it pairs beautifully with various cocktail ingredients, making it a versatile choice for mixologists.

3. American Bourbon: Made primarily from corn and aged in new charred oak barrels, bourbon is a quintessential American whiskey. Its rich and sweet flavors, often with hints of caramel and vanilla, make it a popular choice for classic cocktails like the Old Fashioned and the Mint Julep.

4. Rye Whiskey: Known for its spicy and robust character, rye whiskey is a staple in many classic cocktails. With a higher percentage of rye

grain in the mash bill, it offers a distinct flavor profile that adds depth and complexity to drinks like the Manhattan and the Sazerac.

5. Japanese Whisky: Inspired by Scotch whisky production methods, Japanese whisky has gained international recognition for its exceptional quality. With a focus on craftsmanship and attention to detail, Japanese distillers create a range of styles, from light and delicate to rich and smoky.

Understanding the characteristics of each whiskey type allows bartenders and enthusiasts to create exquisite cocktails that highlight the unique flavors of these spirits. From classic cocktails like the Whiskey Sour and the Boulevardier to tropical creations like the Tiki Whiskey Punch, the possibilities are endless.

Whether you prefer the bold flavors of Scotch whisky or the smoothness of Irish whiskey, exploring the diverse world of whiskey is an adventure in itself. So, grab a glass, experiment with different styles, and embark on a journey through the tropical paradise of exotic whiskey cocktails. Cheers to the art of mixology and the pleasure of enjoying a perfectly crafted whiskey drink, no matter the occasion or season.

Whiskey Sour: A Classic Whiskey Cocktail

The Whiskey Sour is a true classic in the world of cocktails, offering a perfect balance of sweet and sour flavors that has stood the test of time. Whether you're a fan of classic cocktails, tropical concoctions, or signature drinks, the Whiskey Sour is a must-try for any avid drinker. In this chapter, we explore the origins of this timeless libation and provide a step-by-step guide on how to make the perfect Whiskey Sour.

Dating back to the mid-19th century, the Whiskey Sour has a rich history that can be traced back to the United States. This cocktail became particularly popular during the Prohibition era when whiskey was readily available, thanks to the abundance of bootlegged spirits. Today, it remains a staple in bars and lounges worldwide, offering a refreshing and satisfying drink for whiskey enthusiasts.

To make a classic Whiskey Sour, you'll need just a few simple ingredients: whiskey, lemon juice, sugar, and optionally, an egg white for a velvety texture. The key to a great Whiskey Sour lies in the balance of the ingredients. The lemon juice provides a refreshing tang, while the sugar adds a touch of sweetness to counterbalance the tartness. The addition of whiskey gives the cocktail its distinct character and depth.

For those looking for a tropical twist, you can experiment with different types of whiskey, such as bourbon or rye, to add unique flavors to your Whiskey Sour. You can also consider adding a splash of tropical fruit juice, like pineapple or passionfruit, to transport your taste buds to a sun-soaked paradise.

If you prefer non-alcoholic options, fear not! We've also included a variation of the Whiskey Sour called the Mocktail Sour, which substitutes whiskey with a delicious non-alcoholic alternative. This allows everyone, regardless of their drinking preferences, to enjoy the delightful flavors of a Whiskey Sour.

In this chapter, we'll also explore how to create seasonal variations of the Whiskey Sour, perfect for different holidays and occasions throughout the year. From cozy winter flavors to refreshing summer twists, you'll find a Whiskey Sour recipe to suit every season.

So, whether you're a fan of classic cocktails, tropical libations, or exploring unique craft creations, the Whiskey Sour is a versatile and timeless choice. With its perfect balance of sweet and sour flavors, this classic whiskey cocktail is sure to transport you to a tropical paradise with every sip. Cheers to the Whiskey Sour, a drink that has truly stood the test of time!

Manhattan: The Quintessential Whiskey Drink

When it comes to classic cocktails, few can rival the sophistication and timeless allure of the Manhattan. This iconic drink has been a favorite among whiskey enthusiasts for generations, known for its rich and complex flavors that perfectly encapsulate the spirit of Manhattan itself.

The origins of the Manhattan can be traced back to the late 19th century, where it was first concocted at the Manhattan Club in New York. Since then, it has become a staple in bars and lounges around the world, celebrated for its smoothness and versatility.

The key to a great Manhattan lies in its ingredients. Traditionally, it is made with rye whiskey, sweet vermouth, and a dash of aromatic bitters. However, variations using bourbon or even Canadian whiskey have also become popular over the years, allowing drinkers to customize the drink to their taste preferences.

To make a classic Manhattan, start by chilling a mixing glass with ice. Pour in two ounces of your preferred whiskey, followed by one ounce of sweet vermouth. Add a dash or two of bitters, and gently stir the mixture for about 30 seconds to combine the flavors. Strain the drink into a chilled cocktail glass and garnish with a cherry or a twist of orange peel.

The result is a drink that exudes elegance and sophistication. The sweetness of the vermouth is perfectly balanced by the boldness of the whiskey, creating a harmonious blend of flavors that dance on the palate. Sipping on a Manhattan is like taking a journey through time, as you transport yourself to the glamorous era of the 1920s.

The Manhattan is not only a beloved classic, but it also serves as a foundation for many other whiskey-based cocktails. Mixologists have taken this timeless drink and infused it with their own creative twists, resulting in a wide range of variations to explore.

Whether you're a seasoned whiskey connoisseur or a casual drinker looking to expand your cocktail repertoire, the Manhattan is a must-try. Its smooth and sophisticated flavors will transport you to the bustling streets of Manhattan, even if you're sipping it on a tropical beach. So raise your glass, and toast to the quintessential whiskey drink – the Manhattan. Cheers!

Old Fashioned: A Timeless Whiskey Classic

In the world of cocktails, there are few drinks as iconic and revered as the Old Fashioned. This timeless whiskey classic has stood the test of time and continues to captivate drinkers with its rich history and unparalleled flavor. Whether you're a fan of classic cocktails, tropical concoctions, or seasonal delights, the Old Fashioned deserves a special place in your bartender's guide.

The Old Fashioned is a cocktail that traces its origins back to the early 19th century. It was originally crafted as a simple blend of whiskey, sugar, water, and bitters. Over the years, it has evolved and adapted to suit different tastes and preferences. However, the essence of the Old Fashioned remains intact – a perfect balance of flavors that showcases the beauty of whiskey.

What sets the Old Fashioned apart from other cocktails is its simplicity. It highlights the quality and character of the whiskey, making it a favorite among whiskey enthusiasts. The choice of whiskey is crucial in creating the perfect Old Fashioned. Whether you prefer a smooth bourbon, a smoky Scotch, or a spicy rye, each whiskey brings its unique personality to the drink.

To make an Old Fashioned, start by muddling a sugar cube with a few dashes of bitters until it dissolves. Add a splash of water to help incorporate the flavors. Next, add your choice of whiskey and stir gently to mix everything together. Finish off with a twist of citrus peel and a maraschino cherry for a touch of sweetness.

The beauty of the Old Fashioned lies in its versatility. While the traditional recipe remains timeless, mixologists have been experimenting with different variations to create exciting twists on this classic cocktail. From tropical variations that incorporate fresh fruits and exotic spices to seasonal adaptations that showcase the flavors of different holidays, there is an Old Fashioned for every occasion.

So, whether you're a fan of classic cocktails, tropical delights, or seasonal sips, don't forget to add the Old Fashioned to your bartender's guide. Its timeless appeal and exquisite taste make it a must-have in any cocktail repertoire. Cheers to the Old Fashioned – a whiskey classic that will never go out of style.

Mint Julep: A Refreshing Bourbon Delight

The Mint Julep is a classic cocktail that has stood the test of time. Originating in the southern United States, this refreshing bourbon delight has become a favorite among drinkers all over the world. Known for its combination of smooth bourbon, fresh mint leaves, and crushed ice, the Mint Julep is the perfect drink to transport you to a tropical paradise.

In the subchapter, "Mint Julep: A Refreshing Bourbon Delight," we delve into the art of creating this iconic cocktail. Whether you are a classic cocktail enthusiast, a lover of tropical flavors, or simply enjoy indulging in signature drinks, the Mint Julep is a must-try for any bartender or drink connoisseur.

For those who appreciate the craftsmanship of a well-made cocktail, the Mint Julep offers a unique blend of flavors and textures. The rich, caramel notes of bourbon are perfectly balanced by the vibrant freshness of muddled mint leaves. Served over crushed ice, this cocktail provides a cooling sensation that is both invigorating and satisfying.

For those seeking a non-alcoholic option, we also explore the world of mocktails. By substituting bourbon with a high-quality non-alcoholic spirit, you can still enjoy the refreshing taste of a Mint Julep without the alcohol content. Perfect for those looking to indulge in flavorful creations without compromising their sobriety.

Furthermore, we cater to the whiskey enthusiasts in our audience. As a bourbon-based cocktail, the Mint Julep showcases the versatility and complexity of this beloved spirit. Whether you are a fan of smoky peat flavors or prefer the smoothness of a well-aged bourbon, the Mint Julep can be adapted to suit your whiskey preferences.

Additionally, as a bartender's guide, we understand the importance of seasonal offerings. In this subchapter, we explore variations of the Mint Julep that are tailored to different seasons and holidays. From a refreshing summer twist with the addition of fresh berries to a cozy winter rendition infused with cinnamon and cloves, there is a Mint Julep for every occasion.

Indulge in the refreshing flavors of the Mint Julep and allow yourself to be transported to a tropical paradise. Whether you are a classic cocktail lover, a whiskey aficionado, or simply someone seeking a refreshing drink, the Mint Julep is sure to delight your taste buds and leave you longing for more. Join us on this journey as we uncover the secrets behind creating the perfect Mint Julep and explore its endless possibilities. Cheers!

Irish Coffee: A Warming Whiskey Beverage

Irish Coffee is a classic cocktail that combines the rich flavors of coffee and whiskey, creating a warming and indulgent beverage perfect for those chilly evenings. This delightful concoction is a staple in any bartender's arsenal, offering a unique twist on traditional coffee and providing a perfect balance of flavors.

To create an authentic Irish Coffee, you'll need a few key ingredients: freshly brewed hot coffee, Irish whiskey, brown sugar, and heavy cream. The combination of these elements produces a delightful blend of flavors that will transport you to a tropical paradise, even on the coldest of nights.

Start by warming your glass, as this will help maintain the temperature of the drink. Then, dissolve a teaspoon of brown sugar in a little hot water at the bottom of the glass. Next, pour in a shot of Irish whiskey, allowing it to mix with the sugar mixture. Gently pour in the hot coffee, leaving about an inch of space at the top.

Now comes the fun part – the cream. Take a spoon and carefully pour the heavy cream over the back of it, allowing it to float on top of the coffee. This creates a visually appealing layered effect and adds a luxurious touch to the drink. The cream should not be mixed; instead, it is meant to be sipped through, providing a velvety texture and a creamy counterpoint to the bold flavors of the coffee and whiskey.

Irish Coffee is a versatile drink that can be enjoyed year-round. During the colder months, it serves as a comforting and warming beverage, while in the summer, it can be transformed into a refreshing iced version. You can also add a dash of cinnamon or nutmeg on top for an extra touch of flavor and aroma.

Whether you're a fan of classic cocktails, tropical drinks, or whiskey-based beverages, Irish Coffee is a must-try for any discerning drinker. Its combination of rich coffee, smooth whiskey, and creamy indulgence is sure to transport you to a tropical paradise, no matter where you are. So, grab your favorite Irish whiskey and a freshly brewed cup of joe, and enjoy this delightful beverage that truly captures the spirit of relaxation and indulgence.

Whiskey Smash: A Herbaceous Whiskey Cocktail

Whiskey lovers rejoice! The Whiskey Smash is a delightful and refreshing cocktail that combines the bold flavors of whiskey with the herbaceous notes of fresh mint and zesty citrus. This classic cocktail is a must-try for any whiskey aficionado looking to explore new flavor profiles.

The Whiskey Smash is a versatile drink that can be enjoyed year-round, making it a perfect addition to your cocktail repertoire. Whether you're sipping it on a warm summer evening or cozying up by the fire during the winter months, this cocktail will transport you to a tropical paradise with every sip.

To create the perfect Whiskey Smash, start by muddling a handful of fresh mint leaves and a few slices of juicy lemon or lime in a mixing glass. This will release the aromatic oils and flavors of the herbs, infusing your cocktail with a burst of freshness. Next, add your favorite whiskey – whether it's a smooth bourbon or a smoky scotch, the choice is yours. Add a touch of simple syrup or agave nectar to balance the flavors and give the cocktail a touch of sweetness.

Once all the ingredients are in the mixing glass, fill it with ice and shake vigorously to ensure all the flavors are well combined. Strain the mixture into a chilled glass filled with crushed ice, and garnish with a sprig of fresh mint and a citrus twist for an extra burst of aroma.

The Whiskey Smash is a drink that can be easily customized to suit your taste preferences. Experiment with different types of whiskey, such as rye or Irish whiskey, to add unique flavor profiles to your cocktail. For a tropical twist, consider adding a splash of pineapple or passion fruit juice to the mix. The possibilities are endless, and the result is always a delicious and satisfying cocktail.

So, whether you're a whiskey connoisseur or simply looking to expand your cocktail horizons, the Whiskey Smash is a must-try. Its herbaceous flavors, combined with the richness of whiskey, make it a perfect choice for any occasion. Cheers to exploring the world of tropical cocktails and finding your own slice of paradise in every sip!

Whiskey Highball: A Simple and Refreshing Whiskey Mix

If you're a fan of classic cocktails and are looking for a refreshing twist on your favorite whiskey, look no further than the Whiskey Highball. This simple yet delightful drink is perfect for those who appreciate the smoothness and complexity of whiskey but also crave a light and refreshing beverage.

The Whiskey Highball is a versatile cocktail that can be enjoyed year-round, making it a must-have in your bartender's repertoire. Whether you're sipping it on a sunny beach or cozying up by the fire during the winter months, this drink is sure to transport you to a tropical paradise with its exotic flavors.

To create the perfect Whiskey Highball, start with a high-quality whiskey of your choice. The rich and distinctive flavors of whiskey are beautifully complemented by the addition of sparkling water or soda. This combination not only adds a refreshing fizz but also helps to mellow out the intensity of the whiskey, making it more approachable for those who are new to this spirit.

To take your Whiskey Highball to the next level, consider adding a splash of fruit juice or a squeeze of citrus. This will add a burst of flavor and brightness to the drink, elevating it to a whole new level of deliciousness. Experiment with different combinations such as pineapple juice for a tropical twist, or cranberry juice for a festive touch during the holiday season.

For those who prefer non-alcoholic options, the Whiskey Highball can easily be transformed into a mocktail. Simply substitute the whiskey with a non-alcoholic alternative such as a botanical spirit or flavored syrup, and enjoy all the refreshing flavors without the alcohol content.

Whether you're a fan of classic cocktails, tropical flavors, or seasonal drinks, the Whiskey Highball is a versatile and refreshing choice that will transport you to a tropical paradise with every sip. So grab your favorite whiskey, mix it with some sparkling water or soda, and let this simple yet delightful concoction whisk you away to a world of exotic flavors and relaxation. Cheers!

Rusty Nail: A Scotch-Based Whiskey Cocktail

In the world of classic cocktails, there are few drinks that can transport you to a tropical paradise quite like the Rusty Nail. This scotch-based whiskey cocktail is a favorite among bartenders and drink enthusiasts alike, as it combines the rich and smoky flavors of scotch with a touch of sweetness. Whether you're a fan of classic cocktails or looking to explore the world of tropical drinks, the Rusty Nail is a must-try.

To make this exquisite cocktail, you'll need just two simple ingredients: scotch whiskey and Drambuie, a honey and herb-infused liqueur. The combination of these two spirits creates a unique and complex flavor profile that is sure to impress even the most discerning palates.

Start by filling a glass with ice, then pour in equal parts scotch whiskey and Drambuie. Give it a gentle stir to combine the flavors and allow the ice to dilute the drink slightly. The result is a smooth and velvety cocktail that is perfect for sipping on a warm summer evening or cozying up by the fireplace during the colder months.

The Rusty Nail is a versatile cocktail that can be enjoyed year-round. For a tropical twist, garnish your drink with a slice of fresh pineapple or a sprig of mint. If you prefer a more classic presentation, a lemon twist or a maraschino cherry will do the trick.

This cocktail is not only a favorite among whiskey enthusiasts, but also a go-to choice for those looking to explore the world of craft cocktails. Its simplicity allows for endless experimentation, so don't be afraid to get creative and add your own personal touch. Whether you're hosting a cocktail party, enjoying a nightcap, or simply looking to unwind with a delicious drink, the Rusty Nail is sure to transport you to a tropical paradise with every sip.

So grab your favorite scotch whiskey, a bottle of Drambuie, and embark on a flavor journey that combines the best of classic and tropical cocktails. The Rusty Nail is a true gem in the world of whiskey cocktails and a must-have addition to any bartender's repertoire. Cheers to exotic flavors and unforgettable experiences!

Boulevardier: A Whiskey Twist on a Negroni

In the world of classic cocktails, the Negroni stands tall as a beloved and time-honored favorite. But what if we told you there was a way to elevate this iconic drink even further? Enter the Boulevardier, a whiskey twist on the Negroni that adds a whole new dimension of flavor and sophistication.

The Boulevardier is the perfect fusion of two beloved spirits: whiskey and Campari. By replacing the gin in a traditional Negroni with your favorite whiskey, you create a cocktail that is rich, complex, and utterly delicious. The robust and smoky notes of the whiskey complement the bitter and herbal flavors of the Campari, resulting in a drink that is both familiar and excitingly different.

To make a Boulevardier, you'll need just three simple ingredients: whiskey, sweet vermouth, and Campari. Start by combining equal parts of each ingredient in a mixing glass filled with ice. Stir gently to chill the drink without diluting it too much. Strain the mixture into a chilled rocks glass filled with fresh ice and garnish with a twist of orange peel.

The beauty of the Boulevardier is its versatility. You can experiment with different types of whiskey to find your preferred flavor profile. Whether you choose a smooth and mellow bourbon, a peaty and smoky scotch, or a spicy and complex rye, each variation will bring its own unique characteristics to the cocktail.

For whiskey enthusiasts, the Boulevardier offers a delightful departure from the usual whiskey cocktails. Its bitter and herbal notes make it an excellent choice for those who appreciate the complexity of flavors. And for those who are new to whiskey, the Boulevardier provides a gentle introduction, allowing you to ease into the world of this beloved spirit.

Whether you're sipping a Boulevardier on a tropical beach, enjoying it as a signature cocktail at a craft cocktail bar, or savoring it as a seasonal libation for a holiday celebration, this whiskey twist on a Negroni is sure to transport you to a tropical paradise of flavor and enjoyment. So grab your favorite bottle of whiskey and embark on a cocktail adventure with the Boulevardier – you won't be disappointed. Cheers!

Whiskey Ginger: A Spicy and Refreshing Whiskey Blend

If you're a fan of classic cocktails with a twist, the Whiskey Ginger is the perfect drink to add to your repertoire. This spicy and refreshing whiskey blend will transport you to a tropical paradise with every sip.

Whether you're a seasoned whiskey connoisseur or just looking to try something new, the Whiskey Ginger is sure to delight your taste buds.

To make this tantalizing cocktail, you'll need just a few simple ingredients. Start with a high-quality whiskey of your choice – whether you prefer a smooth bourbon or a peaty scotch, the choice is yours. Combine this with the zing of fresh ginger, a hint of lime juice, and a touch of sweetness from simple syrup or ginger syrup. Shake it all up with ice and strain into a glass filled with fresh ice. Garnish with a slice of lime or a sprig of mint, and you're ready to enjoy a taste of tropical paradise.

The Whiskey Ginger is a versatile drink that can be enjoyed year-round. In the heat of summer, it provides a refreshing escape from the sweltering sun. The spicy kick of ginger adds a unique twist to the classic whiskey taste, making it a perfect choice for those looking to spice up their cocktail game.

For bartenders who specialize in classic cocktails, the Whiskey Ginger is a must-have in your repertoire. Its simplicity makes it easy to prepare, yet its bold flavors make it a standout on any menu. By offering this unique twist on a traditional whiskey drink, you'll satisfy the palates of both whiskey aficionados and those seeking a new and exciting taste experience.

For those who prefer non-alcoholic options, the Whiskey Ginger can easily be transformed into a mocktail. Simply replace the whiskey with a non-alcoholic alternative, such as ginger ale or ginger beer, and you'll still be able to enjoy the spicy and refreshing flavors of this tropical-inspired blend.

No matter the occasion or season, the Whiskey Ginger is a versatile and crowd-pleasing cocktail that will transport you to a tropical paradise.

So, gather your ingredients, shake up a glass, and let the flavors whisk you away to an exotic destination with every sip. Cheers!

Chapter 6: Craft Cocktails: A Bartender's Guide

The Art of Craft Cocktails

Welcome to the subchapter titled "The Art of Craft Cocktails" from the book "Tropical Paradise: Exotic Cocktails to Transport Drinkers." Whether you are a seasoned drinker or an aspiring mixologist, this chapter is dedicated to showcasing the intricacies and creativity behind crafting the perfect cocktail.

Craft cocktails have become a phenomenon in recent years, with bartenders around the world pushing the boundaries of mixology. These cocktails are more than just a drink; they are a work of art, combining unique flavors, textures, and presentations to create an unforgettable experience.

In this subchapter, we will explore the techniques, ingredients, and inspiration behind crafting craft cocktails. We will delve into the different niches of cocktail making, including classic cocktails, tropical cocktails, signature cocktails, mocktails, whiskey cocktails, gin cocktails, rum cocktails, vodka cocktails, and seasonal cocktails.

For the lovers of classic cocktails, we will take a journey through time, exploring the origins and evolution of beloved drinks like the Old Fashioned, Martini, and Negroni. Discover the secrets to balancing flavors and perfecting the art of garnishing.

If you're dreaming of a tropical getaway, our tropical cocktail section will transport you to a beach paradise. Learn how to infuse your drinks with exotic fruits, spices, and herbs to create refreshing concoctions that mimic the flavors of the tropics.

For those seeking unique and personalized experiences, our signature cocktail section will provide inspiration and guidance on how to craft your own masterpiece. Unleash your creativity and experiment with unconventional ingredients and techniques to create a drink that reflects your personality.

Non-drinkers need not feel left out, as our mocktail section offers a wide array of non-alcoholic mixed drinks that are just as delicious and visually appealing as their alcoholic counterparts. Discover the art of balancing flavors and creating complex mocktails that cater to everyone's tastes.

Whiskey enthusiasts will find a treasure trove of whiskey cocktail recipes, from the classic Whiskey Sour to innovative creations that highlight the spirit's versatility. Learn how to enhance the flavors of different whiskey varieties and elevate your cocktail game.

Gin, rum, and vodka lovers will also find their thirst quenched with dedicated sections that explore the unique characteristics of these spirits and provide recipes for both classic and innovative cocktails.

Lastly, our seasonal cocktail section will guide you through the year, featuring drinks tailored to different seasons and holidays. From cozy winter warmers to refreshing summer sips, we have you covered all year round.

So, grab your shaker, muddler, and a copy of "Tropical Paradise: Exotic Cocktails to Transport Drinkers," and let's embark on a journey to master the art of craft cocktails. Cheers!

Essential Techniques for Crafting Unique Cocktails

In the world of mixology, the ability to create unique and memorable cocktails is a highly sought-after skill. Whether you're a seasoned bartender or an enthusiastic home mixologist, mastering essential techniques can elevate your cocktail game and transport your drinkers to a tropical paradise. This subchapter of "Tropical Paradise: Exotic Cocktails to Transport Drinkers" will delve into the techniques that will help you create exceptional drinks that cater to the various niches of classic, tropical, signature, mocktails, whiskey, craft, gin, rum, vodka, and seasonal cocktails.

Firstly, let's explore the art of flavor balancing. Understanding the interplay of sweet, sour, bitter, and salty elements is crucial to crafting a well-rounded cocktail. Experiment with different combinations of ingredients, such as citrus juices, simple syrups, bitters, and herbs, to achieve harmonious flavors that tantalize the taste buds. Remember, balance is key!

Next, we'll delve into the importance of using fresh and high-quality ingredients. From ripe fruits to premium spirits, the quality of your ingredients greatly impacts the final outcome of your cocktail. Explore local markets to discover seasonal fruits and experiment with unique spirits to create truly exceptional drinks that showcase the flavors of the tropics.

Mixing techniques are also vital in creating unique cocktails. From shaking to stirring, each technique imparts a different texture and level of dilution to the drink. Learn when to shake vigorously to create a frothy concoction or when to stir gently for a smoother finish. Experiment with different techniques to achieve the desired mouthfeel and presentation.

Presentation and garnishes are the finishing touches that can make your cocktails truly stand out. Whether it's a tropical umbrella, a fresh fruit skewer, or an aromatic herb sprig, the right garnish can enhance the visual appeal and aroma of your drink, transporting your drinkers to a tropical oasis with a single glance.

Lastly, don't be afraid to experiment and push boundaries. The world of mixology is constantly evolving, and creating unique cocktails often requires thinking outside the box. Play with unexpected flavor combinations, infusions, and innovative techniques to surprise and delight your drinkers.

By mastering these essential techniques, you'll be well on your way to crafting unique and memorable cocktails that cater to the diverse preferences of classic cocktail enthusiasts, tropical cocktail lovers, signature cocktail seekers, mocktail drinkers, whiskey connoisseurs, craft cocktail enthusiasts, gin aficionados, rum enthusiasts, vodka lovers, and those in search of seasonal delights. So, grab your shaker, gather your ingredients, and embark on a journey to create tropical paradise in every glass. Cheers!

Craft Margarita Variations

The margarita is a classic cocktail that has stood the test of time. With its refreshing blend of tequila, lime juice, and triple sec, it's no wonder this drink has become a favorite among drinkers worldwide. However, for those looking to add a twist to their margarita experience, craft margarita variations offer a whole new level of creativity and flavor.

In this subchapter, we will explore a range of craft margarita variations that are sure to transport drinkers to a tropical paradise. From unique flavor combinations to innovative presentation techniques, these cocktails are perfect for bartenders looking to impress their guests and elevate their cocktail menu.

For the classic cocktail enthusiasts, we have a selection of traditional margarita variations that stay true to the original recipe while incorporating subtle twists. From the spicy jalapeno margarita to the fruity mango margarita, these variations add an extra kick to the traditional margarita experience.

Tropical cocktail lovers will delight in our selection of exotic margarita variations. With ingredients like coconut, pineapple, and passionfruit, these cocktails capture the essence of a tropical paradise in every sip. Whether you prefer a refreshing coconut margarita or a tangy pineapple margarita, these variations are guaranteed to transport you to a beachside oasis.

For those seeking a unique and signature cocktail experience, our craft margarita variations offer a range of innovative flavor combinations. From the smoky mezcal margarita to the savory bacon-infused margarita, these cocktails push the boundaries of traditional mixology and deliver a truly unforgettable drinking experience.

Non-alcoholic mixed drink enthusiasts will also find something to suit their taste buds in our selection of mocktail margarita variations. From the zesty virgin margarita to the refreshing watermelon mockarita, these alcohol-free options provide all the flavor and excitement of a margarita without the buzz.

Whether you're a fan of whiskey, gin, rum, or vodka, our craft margarita variations have got you covered. With unique twists on these spirits, such as the whiskey barrel-aged margarita or the gin-infused lavender margarita, these variations cater to the diverse tastes of cocktail connoisseurs.

Finally, our seasonal margarita variations offer a selection of drinks for different seasons and holidays. From a spicy pumpkin margarita for Halloween to a refreshing cucumber margarita for the summer, these cocktails celebrate the changing seasons and provide a festive twist to your margarita experience.

In conclusion, craft margarita variations offer a world of possibilities for bartenders and drinkers alike. With their innovative flavor combinations, creative presentation, and unique twists, these cocktails are sure to transport you to a tropical paradise with every sip. So grab a glass, shake up a craft margarita, and let the exotic flavors take you on a journey to cocktail bliss.

Craft Martini Variations

In the world of cocktails, the martini has become an iconic symbol of sophistication and elegance. Its simple yet refined combination of gin and vermouth has captivated drinkers for generations. However, in recent years, mixologists and bartenders have taken this classic cocktail to new heights with their innovative and creative twists. In this subchapter, we explore the world of craft martini variations that are sure to transport you to a tropical paradise.

For those who prefer the exotic flavors of the tropics, we have curated a selection of tropical martini variations that will tickle your taste buds. From the refreshing Pineapple Coconut Martini, with its blend of fresh pineapple juice, coconut rum, and a splash of lime, to the tantalizing Mango Passion Martini, infused with the flavors of ripe mango and passion fruit, these cocktails are the perfect accompaniment to a sunny day by the beach.

If you're a fan of classic cocktails, fear not, for we have not forgotten you. Our craft martini variations also include a range of classic-inspired concoctions that pay homage to the traditional martini while adding a modern twist. The Espresso Martini, for example, combines the rich flavors of coffee liqueur and vodka, creating a delightful pick-me-up cocktail that is perfect for after-dinner indulgence.

For those seeking a non-alcoholic option, our mocktail martini variations will not disappoint. From the Virgin Raspberry Cosmopolitan, featuring a delightful blend of cranberry juice, raspberry syrup, and lime, to the alcohol-free Mojito Martini, infused with the refreshing flavors of mint and lime, these mocktails are both delicious and refreshing.

For the whiskey, rum, vodka, and gin enthusiasts, we have crafted martini variations specifically tailored to each spirit. Whether you prefer the smoky notes of a whiskey martini, the tropical flavors of a rum martini, the crispness of a vodka martini, or the herbal complexities of a gin martini, there is a craft martini variation that is sure to satisfy your palate.

Lastly, we haven't forgotten about seasonal celebrations. Our craft martini variations also include seasonal cocktails that are perfect for different holidays and seasons throughout the year. From the Spiced Pumpkin Martini for Halloween to the Cranberry Mule Martini for Christmas, these cocktails will add a festive touch to any occasion.

So, whether you're a lover of classic cocktails, a tropical aficionado, or simply looking for a new and exciting martini experience, our craft martini variations have something for everyone. Sit back, relax, and let your taste buds be transported to a tropical paradise with every sip. Cheers!

Craft Mojito Variations

The Mojito is a classic cocktail that originated in Cuba and has gained popularity all around the world for its refreshing and vibrant flavors. While the traditional Mojito recipe is delicious on its own, there are countless variations that can take this cocktail to new heights. In this subchapter, we explore the art of crafting unique Mojito variations that will transport drinkers to a tropical paradise.

For the lovers of classic cocktails, we present the Classic Mojito with a Twist. This variation maintains the traditional blend of fresh mint, lime juice, sugar, and rum, but adds a splash of pineapple juice for a sweet and tangy twist. It's the perfect balance between tradition and innovation.

Tropical cocktail enthusiasts will be delighted by the Tropical Mojito Fusion. This variation combines the traditional elements of a Mojito with exotic fruits such as mango, passion fruit, and guava. The result is a tropical explosion of flavors that will transport you to a sun-kissed beach with every sip.

For those seeking signature cocktails, the Signature Mojito Elixir is a must-try. This variation infuses the classic Mojito with elderflower liqueur and a hint of cucumber, creating a sophisticated and aromatic drink that is as elegant as it is delicious.

Non-alcoholic mixed drink aficionados will not be left behind with the Mocktail Mojito Bliss. This alcohol-free variation substitutes rum with sparkling water and adds a splash of cranberry juice for a refreshing and tangy twist. It's the perfect option for those looking for a flavorful and alcohol-free alternative.

Whiskey lovers can also enjoy the best of both worlds with the Whiskey Mojito Fusion. This variation replaces rum with a smooth and smoky whiskey, adding a unique twist to the traditional Mojito recipe. The combination of whiskey, mint, and lime creates a complex and satisfying flavor profile that will captivate whiskey connoisseurs.

Craft Mojito Variations is a subchapter that caters to the diverse tastes and preferences of drinkers. Whether you're a fan of classic cocktails, tropical delights, signature creations, or non-alcoholic options, there's a Mojito variation for everyone. So grab your shaker, muddle some fresh mint leaves, and embark on a journey through the tropical paradise of Mojito variations. Cheers to endless possibilities!

Craft Old Fashioned Variations

Crafting old fashioned variations is a delightful way to explore the rich history and flavors of classic cocktails. In this subchapter, we will delve into the art of reinventing the timeless old fashioned cocktail with a tropical twist.

For the discerning drinkers who appreciate the elegance of classic cocktails, this section will provide a fresh take on the beloved old fashioned. By infusing it with tropical flavors, we transport you to a lush paradise where every sip feels like a vacation.

In "Tropical Paradise: Exotic Cocktails to Transport Drinkers," we have carefully curated a collection of old fashioned variations that will tantalize your taste buds. Each recipe is thoughtfully crafted to showcase the flavors of the tropics while paying homage to the traditional old fashioned.

Our bartenders' expertise shines through in these innovative concoctions. Whether you are a fan of whiskey, rum, gin, or vodka, we have a tropical old fashioned variation that will suit your preferences. From the smoky depths of a pineapple-infused whiskey old fashioned to the refreshing burst of citrus in a coconut rum old fashioned, there is something for every palate.

For those seeking a non-alcoholic option, we have included a mocktail version of the tropical old fashioned. With the same attention to flavors and presentation, these alcohol-free mixed drinks are perfect for anyone looking for a sophisticated and refreshing alternative.

We also understand the importance of seasonal and holiday-inspired cocktails. That's why we have included a range of old fashioned variations that feature flavors and ingredients specifically tailored to different seasons and holidays. From a spiced apple old fashioned for fall to a vibrant strawberry basil old fashioned for summer, these seasonal delights will elevate your cocktail game year-round.

Whether you are a seasoned bartender or an enthusiastic home mixologist, "Craft Old Fashioned Variations" is a chapter that will inspire and delight. So grab your shaker, muddle some fresh fruit, and embark on a tropical journey through the world of old fashioned cocktails. Cheers to a taste of paradise!

Craft Collins Variations

In the world of cocktails, the Collins is a classic that has stood the test of time. Its refreshing combination of spirits, citrus, and soda water has made it a staple in bars around the globe. But why stick to the traditional recipe when you can explore a world of delicious variations? In this subchapter, we present to you a collection of Craft Collins variations that will transport your taste buds to a tropical paradise.

For the fans of classic cocktails, our Craft Collins variations offer a twist on the traditional recipe. How about a Mango Collins, where the tangy sweetness of mango complements the bright citrus notes perfectly? Or perhaps a Pineapple Collins, with its tropical flavor profile that will transport you to a sunny beach with just one sip.

If you're in the mood for something truly exotic, our Tropical Collins variations are sure to please. Picture yourself sipping on a Passionfruit Collins, where the vibrant flavor of passionfruit takes center stage. Or indulge in a Guava Collins, where the distinctive taste of guava adds a touch of the tropics to your glass.

For those seeking unique and innovative cocktails, our Signature Collins variations are a must-try. How about a Cucumber Collins, where the cool and crisp taste of cucumber adds a refreshing twist? Or perhaps a Lavender Collins, where the delicate floral notes of lavender create a truly elegant cocktail experience.

If you prefer non-alcoholic options, our Mocktail Collins variations are here to satisfy your cravings. From a Virgin Berry Collins bursting with fresh berries to a zesty Lemon Lime Collins, these alcohol-free alternatives are just as delicious and refreshing as their boozy counterparts.

For the whiskey enthusiasts, our Whiskey Collins variations will take your love for this spirit to new heights. Try a Blackberry Whiskey Collins, where the richness of blackberries pairs harmoniously with the smoothness of whiskey. Or experiment with a Maple Bourbon Collins, where the sweetness of maple syrup elevates the classic Collins to new levels of indulgence.

No cocktail guide would be complete without options for gin, rum, vodka, and seasonal cocktails. Our Craft Collins variations cover it all. Discover the botanical delights of a Rosemary Gin Collins or the tropical escapism of a Coconut Rum Collins. And when the seasons change, delight in the cozy flavors of a Spiced Apple Collins or the festive cheer of a Cranberry Orange Collins.

In this subchapter, we invite you to embark on a journey through the world of Craft Collins variations. Whether you're a lover of classic cocktails, tropical flavors, or seasonal delights, there's a Collins variation waiting to transport you to a tropical paradise. Cheers to the art of crafting the perfect cocktail!

Craft Negroni Variations

The Negroni is a classic cocktail that has stood the test of time. With its perfect balance of bitter Campari, sweet vermouth, and strong gin, it has become a favorite among cocktail enthusiasts. But why settle for the traditional recipe when you can explore a world of Negroni variations that will transport your taste buds to a tropical paradise?

In this subchapter, we will take a deep dive into the art of crafting Negroni variations that will delight drinkers from all walks of life.

Whether you're a fan of classic cocktails, tropical concoctions, or signature drinks, there's a Negroni variation for you.

For those seeking a taste of the tropics, why not try a Tropical Negroni? Swap out the traditional gin for a premium rum, add a splash of pineapple juice, and garnish with a fresh slice of pineapple. This variation will transport you to a sandy beach, with the warm breeze and the sound of crashing waves.

If you're a whiskey lover, the Whiskey Negroni is a must-try. Replace the gin with your favorite whiskey, add a dash of orange bitters, and garnish with an orange twist. The rich and smoky flavors of the whiskey will elevate this classic cocktail to new heights.

For those looking for a non-alcoholic option, the Mocktail Negroni is the perfect choice. Simply replace the gin with a botanical-infused non-alcoholic spirit, and add a splash of grapefruit juice. Garnish with a sprig of rosemary for an aromatic twist. This refreshing drink is perfect for those who want to enjoy the flavors of a Negroni without the alcohol.

And let's not forget about seasonal variations. In the subchapter, you'll find Negroni recipes tailored to different seasons and holidays. From a Spiced Negroni for cozy winter nights to a Fruity Negroni Punch for summer parties, there's a Negroni variation to suit every occasion.

So grab your shaker and start experimenting with these craft Negroni variations. Whether you're a fan of classic cocktails, tropical flavors, or seasonal creations, there's a Negroni variation waiting to transport you to a tropical paradise. Cheers to the art of crafting the perfect cocktail!

Craft Sour Variations

In the world of mixology, the sour cocktail is a timeless classic that never fails to impress. Its perfect balance of sweet, sour, and strong flavors has made it a favorite among bartenders and drinkers alike. In this subchapter, we explore the art of crafting sour variations that will transport you to a tropical paradise.

For those who prefer the traditional, we start with the classic Whiskey Sour. This simple yet sophisticated cocktail combines the richness of whiskey with the tanginess of fresh lemon juice and the sweetness of simple syrup. The result is a smooth and refreshing drink that is sure to please any whiskey lover.

Moving on to tropical flavors, we delve into the world of rum cocktails. The Tropical Sour takes the traditional sour and adds a delightful twist of pineapple juice and coconut cream. The result is a creamy and tropical concoction that will transport you to a sandy beach with every sip.

If gin is your spirit of choice, the Gin Sour is a must-try. By adding a touch of elderflower liqueur and fresh cucumber juice, this variation elevates the classic sour to new heights. The crispness of the gin combined with the floral and refreshing notes of elderflower and cucumber create a sophisticated and unique cocktail experience.

For vodka enthusiasts, the Vodka Sour offers a refreshing take on the traditional sour. By infusing the vodka with fresh strawberries and adding a splash of lime juice, this variation adds a fruity and tangy twist to the classic recipe. The result is a vibrant and delicious cocktail that is perfect for any occasion.

Finally, for those looking for non-alcoholic options, we offer a Mocktail Sour variation. By replacing the spirits with a combination of citrus juices, simple syrup, and soda water, this mocktail retains the classic sour flavor profile while remaining alcohol-free. It's a refreshing and satisfying option for those who prefer to skip the booze.

Whether you're a fan of classic cocktails, tropical flavors, or seasonal variations, the craft sour variations in this subchapter will transport you to a tropical paradise with every sip. So grab your shaker and get ready to elevate your cocktail game with these enticing and flavorful creations. Cheers!

Craft Mule Variations

In the world of craft cocktails, there is one drink that has become a timeless classic: the Moscow Mule. This refreshing and tangy cocktail, made with vodka, ginger beer, and lime juice, has been a favorite among drinkers for decades. But what if we told you that there are endless variations of this beloved drink? Welcome to the world of Craft Mule Variations!

Whether you're a fan of classic cocktails, tropical flavors, or signature creations, Craft Mule Variations has something for everyone. In this subchapter, we will explore the diverse and exciting ways to reinvent the Moscow Mule and take your taste buds on a journey to a tropical paradise.

For those who love the classics, we present the Classic Mule Twist. By simply adding a splash of your favorite fruit liqueur, such as peach or raspberry, you can elevate the traditional Moscow Mule to new heights. The combination of the ginger beer's spice, the vodka's smoothness, and the fruity sweetness creates a drink that is both familiar and surprising.

If you're a fan of tropical cocktails, we have the Tropical Mule Fusion. By swapping out the traditional vodka for a tropical rum, such as coconut or pineapple-infused rum, you can transport yourself to a beachfront paradise with just one sip. The addition of fresh tropical fruits, like mango or passionfruit, adds a burst of flavor that will make you feel like you're lounging under a palm tree.

For those looking for a non-alcoholic option, we have the Mocktail Mule. By substituting the vodka with a non-alcoholic spirit, such as Seedlip or Ritual, and using a ginger beer with a kick, you can enjoy the refreshing flavors of a Moscow Mule without the alcohol. Perfect for designated drivers or those who prefer a booze-free option.

Craft Mule Variations also caters to whiskey, gin, and vodka enthusiasts, with unique twists that showcase the versatility of these spirits. And for those who love to celebrate different seasons and holidays, we have a selection of seasonal mules that feature ingredients and flavors that are perfect for each occasion.

So, grab your shaker and prepare to embark on a delicious adventure with Craft Mule Variations. With its wide range of flavors and endless possibilities, this subchapter is a must-have for any bartender or cocktail enthusiast looking to transport their drinkers to a tropical paradise, one sip at a time. Cheers!

Craft Punch Variations

In the world of cocktails, punches have always held a special place. These delightful concoctions bring people together, creating a sense of camaraderie and celebration. And what better way to transport yourself to a tropical paradise than with a refreshing craft punch? In this subchapter, we explore the art of crafting punch variations that will tantalize your taste buds and transport you to exotic destinations.

For the classic cocktail enthusiasts, we present the Classic Punch Revamp. Taking inspiration from traditional recipes, we add a modern twist with tropical fruits and artisanal spirits. Sip on this timeless favorite and let the flavors of the islands dance on your palate.

For those seeking a taste of the tropics, our Tropical Punch Extravaganza is a must-try. Bursting with the vibrant flavors of pineapple, mango, and coconut, this punch will transport you to a beachside paradise with every sip. Garnish with a colorful umbrella, and you'll feel like you're lounging under palm trees.

If you're looking to impress your guests with a signature creation, look no further than our Signature Punch Spectacular. This unique blend combines unexpected ingredients and innovative techniques to create a punch that is truly one-of-a-kind. Experiment with herbs, spices, and homemade infusions to add a personal touch to your creation.

For those who prefer non-alcoholic options, our Mocktail Punch Bonanza offers a range of refreshing and flavorful punches that can be enjoyed by everyone. From fruity mocktails to herb-infused spritzers, these alcohol-free options are perfect for any occasion.

Whiskey lovers will find solace in our Whiskey Punch Elixir. The rich and smoky flavors of whiskey are complemented by a medley of citrus and spices, creating a punch that is both robust and sophisticated. Served over ice, this punch is sure to be a crowd-pleaser.

Gin enthusiasts can indulge in our Gin Punch Delight. With its botanical notes and crisp flavors, gin is the perfect base for a refreshing punch. Add a splash of citrus and a hint of herbs to create a drink that is both elegant and refreshing.

Rum aficionados will find their paradise in our Rum Punch Bliss. This tropical elixir combines the smoothness of rum with the sweetness of tropical fruits, creating a punch that is both indulgent and irresistible. Served in a coconut shell, this punch is a true taste of the islands.

Vodka lovers need not be left out with our Vodka Punch Sensation. This versatile spirit pairs perfectly with a variety of fruits and flavors, allowing you to create a punch that suits your taste. Whether you prefer a citrus-infused punch or a berry-filled delight, vodka is the ideal base for your craft punch creation.

And finally, for those who love to celebrate the changing seasons and holidays, our Seasonal Punch Extravaganza offers a range of festive punches to suit every occasion. From spiced apple cider punches for cozy winter nights to refreshing watermelon punches for hot summer days, these seasonal delights will keep your guests entertained all year round.

With these craft punch variations, we invite you to embark on a journey of taste and imagination. Let the flavors of these exotic cocktails transport you to a tropical paradise, no matter where you may be. Cheers to the art of craft punch!

Craft Spritz Variations

In the world of cocktails, the spritz has been a beloved classic for decades. Its refreshing and bubbly nature makes it the perfect drink for any occasion, whether you're lounging by the pool or enjoying a night out with friends. In this subchapter, we will explore some exciting variations of the traditional spritz that will transport you to a tropical paradise.

For those who prefer a more tropical twist, the Tropical Spritz is a must-try. Combining the flavors of pineapple, coconut, and lime, this cocktail will instantly transport you to a beachside getaway. The addition of rum adds a delightful kick that perfectly complements the fruity flavors.

If you're looking for a lighter and healthier option, the Sparkling Citrus Spritz is the way to go. This mocktail combines the zesty flavors of grapefruit and orange with a splash of sparkling water, creating a refreshing and revitalizing drink. It's the perfect choice for those who want to enjoy a delicious cocktail without the alcohol.

For whiskey lovers, the Whiskey Ginger Spritz is a game-changer. This variation combines the rich and smoky flavors of whiskey with the spicy kick of ginger beer. Topped off with a squeeze of fresh lemon juice and a sprig of mint, this cocktail is a true crowd-pleaser.

Gin enthusiasts will delight in the Herb-infused Gin Spritz. By infusing your gin with herbs like rosemary, thyme, or basil, you can create a unique and aromatic cocktail experience. Add a splash of tonic water and a garnish of fresh herbs, and you have a spritz that is as visually appealing as it is delicious.

No cocktail guide would be complete without a vodka-based option. The Cucumber Melon Spritz is a light and refreshing choice, perfect for those hot summer days. Combining the crisp flavors of cucumber and melon with a splash of soda water, this cocktail is a true delight for the taste buds.

Whether you're a fan of classic cocktails, tropical flavors, or seasonal specialties, these craft spritz variations are sure to impress. Experiment with different ingredients, garnishes, and techniques to create your own unique twist on the spritz. Cheers to a tropical paradise in every sip!

Chapter 7: Gin Cocktails: A Bartender's Guide

Introduction to Gin Cocktails

Welcome to the world of gin cocktails, where the refreshing and aromatic flavors of this beloved spirit take center stage. In this subchapter, we will explore the art of crafting exquisite gin-based concoctions that are sure to transport your taste buds to a tropical paradise. Whether you are a seasoned gin enthusiast or new to the world of cocktails, this guide is designed to appeal to a wide range of drinkers.

Gin, with its unique blend of botanicals, has a rich history dating back centuries. Its versatility and ability to complement a variety of flavors make it a favorite among mixologists. In this subchapter, we will delve into the fascinating origins of gin, its production methods, and the various styles available to bartenders and cocktail enthusiasts alike.

But what truly sets gin apart is its ability to shine in a myriad of cocktail creations. From classic cocktails to innovative tropical blends, gin offers a world of possibilities. Whether you prefer the timeless elegance of a Martini, the zesty freshness of a Gin and Tonic, or the exotic allure of a Singapore Sling, gin cocktails are as diverse as the regions they represent.

This subchapter aims to cater to the diverse interests of our readership, including lovers of classic cocktails, tropical concoctions, and signature drinks. We also acknowledge the growing demand for non-alcoholic options, which is why we have included a section on gin-based mocktails for those seeking a refreshing experience without the alcohol content.

In addition to the various styles and cocktail recipes, we will also explore the art of garnishing and presentation, as well as tips and tricks to elevate your gin cocktails to new heights. Whether you are hosting a seasonal gathering, a craft cocktail soirée, or simply looking to unwind with a well-crafted drink after a long day, this subchapter has something for everyone.

So, join us on this journey through the intriguing world of gin cocktails. Let us transport you to a tropical paradise with every sip, as we explore the flavors, techniques, and inspiration behind these delightful libations. Cheers to the endless possibilities that gin cocktails offer, and may your glass always be filled with the taste of paradise.

Essential

Subchapter: Essential

In the world of cocktails, certain ingredients and techniques are considered essential. These elements form the foundation of every great drink, ensuring that every sip is a perfect balance of flavors and textures. In this subchapter, we will explore the essential components that every bartender and drink enthusiast should have in their arsenal. Whether you are a fan of classic cocktails, tropical delights, or innovative signature drinks, mastering these essentials will elevate your mixology game to new heights.

First and foremost, let's talk about the tools of the trade. A well-stocked bar should include a shaker, jigger, muddler, strainer, and a variety of glassware. These tools will enable you to mix, measure, crush, and strain your ingredients with precision, resulting in perfectly crafted cocktails.

Next, let's dive into the must-have ingredients. In the realm of classic cocktails, you can't go wrong with bitters. A few drops of aromatic bitters can transform a drink, adding depth and complexity. Other essentials include citrus fruits like lemons and limes for their zesty freshness, simple syrup for sweetness, and a selection of spirits such as whiskey, gin, rum, and vodka.

For those who prefer tropical cocktails, ingredients like fresh fruit juices (pineapple, mango, and passion fruit), coconut cream, and exotic liqueurs (such as rum-based banana or coconut liqueur) are a must. These ingredients will transport you to a sandy beach with every sip.

In the realm of signature cocktails, the sky's the limit. However, a few essentials remain. Craft cocktail enthusiasts should experiment with homemade infusions, syrups, and garnishes. Fresh herbs like mint, basil, and rosemary add a touch of sophistication, while homemade infusions (think jalapeno-infused tequila or lavender-infused vodka) can take your drink to the next level.

For those seeking a non-alcoholic option, the world of mocktails offers a plethora of exciting choices. Essential ingredients for mocktails include fresh fruits, flavored syrups, and soda water. With a little creativity, you can concoct vibrant and refreshing mocktails that are just as enjoyable as their alcoholic counterparts.

Finally, no bartender's guide would be complete without a section on seasonal cocktails. From festive holiday drinks to refreshing summer sippers, these recipes highlight the best flavors each season has to offer. Essential ingredients for seasonal cocktails include spices like cinnamon and nutmeg, fresh herbs, seasonal fruits, and specialty spirits like apple brandy or spiced rum.

No matter your drink preference, mastering the essentials will allow you to create unforgettable cocktails. So gather your tools, stock up on ingredients, and let your imagination run wild. Cheers to your tropical paradise filled with exotic cocktails!